Eating Pretty

SMART TALK

Eating Pretty

Elizabeth Karlsberg

Troll Associates

ACKNOWLEDGEMENT

A special thanks to Gail Meinhold, R.D. for her time and expert assistance in assuring that the information contained in this book is sound and accurate.

Library of Congress Cataloging-in-Publication Data

Karlsberg, Elizabeth.
 Eating pretty / by Elizabeth Karlsberg; illustrated by Donald Richey.
  p.   cm.—(Smart talk)
  Summary: Advice for young girls on eating nutritionally, not only for health, but for beauty.
  ISBN 0-8167-2001-0 (lib. bdg.)   ISBN 0-8167-2002-9 (pbk.)
  1. Children—Nutrition—Juvenile literature.   2. Nutrition—Examinations, questions, etc.—Juvenile literature.   3. Cookery—Juvenile literature.   [1. Nutrition.]   I. Richey, Donald, ill.
II. Title.   III. Series.
RJ206.K244   1991
613.2'083'4—dc20   89-39935

Table of Contents

Why Worry About What You Eat?

When you think of nutrition, what comes to mind? Boring stuff like calorie counting? Food that's supposed to be good for you but doesn't taste very good? Something that only people who have a weight problem have to worry about? Guess again! Nutrition is about YOU—about everything you eat, or don't eat. It's the cold pizza you sneak at midnight. It's your indestructible appetite for anything sweet. It's hot dogs at a baseball game and Sunday morning pancakes. Nutrition is something that everyone should be concerned about—no matter how young or old they happen to be!

NUTRITION: THE TIME IS NOW!

One thing that most nutrition experts agree on is this: What you eat affects not only how you feel when you're *young*, but how healthy you'll be when you're *older*.

Older? But that's years from now! And that's the exact reason so many young people have a hard time thinking so far ahead. They're healthy, they're active, they're having a good time—so why bother *now* with worries of *later*?

First of all, the effects of poor nutrition don't always wait until you're old and gray to show up. No one claims that if you eat a well-balanced diet you'll be protected from all of the diseases many people get in old age. On the other hand, there's lots of proof that people who don't eat well are less able to fight off infection—even a common cold.

In addition, poor eating habits can make you feel tired and generally yucky. You know how it is when you get a case of the mid-afternoon hungries and can't concentrate on what's happening in class? In a sense, it's similar to when your body doesn't get the good food it needs over a long period of time. It can't function properly. It's like continually driving a car without enough oil in it. Eventually, if you're not careful, the parts get worn down.

Although you can go without food for a short while when you have to, it's not a good idea. Even skipping one meal can throw your body off balance. When you eat healthfully, your motor really gets revving because every food has a purpose—it's not just eaten to fill you up. Better yet, when you service your body by filling 'er up with nutritious foods, you'll perform better—both physically and mentally.

If that doesn't convince you that there's some value to eating well, maybe this will: How you *look*—even in your pre-teen and teen years—is also affected by what you eat!

If you're like most young women, you probably spend lots of time worrying about your looks. Of course, it's better if you don't spend too much time in front of the mirror, but the truth is, looks *do* matter.

You're probably familiar with some version of the following routine:

You get up early, sacrificing precious sleep, just to make sure your mane looks marvelous. After you've moussed, gelled and sprayed your locks into shape, you try on outfit after outfit until you're satisfied that you've found just the right combination of clothes.

And don't forget makeup. If you've already started to wear it, then you put your pretty face in front of a mirror to make it even prettier. There you stand until everything—from lips to lashes—looks absolutely lovely. You may have even painted your fingernails the night before. Everything has to be just right, and only when it is are you finally ready to face the world.

A split-second before you're about to leave to catch the school bus, you hear your mom or dad yell from the other end of the house, "Don't forget about breakfast!"

"Yeah, yeah, yeah," you mutter to yourself. But, so you won't feel too guilty, you decide to grab a quick bite. You search the kitchen for anything that has a plastic wrapper, and settle on a sticky, gooey, sugary something. Pop! it goes—into your mouth. Before you

3

Not a healthy breakfast.

even begin chewing, you check the fridge for something to wash down the delicacy. Milk? Orange juice? The thought doesn't even cross your mind, or if it does, it's for only a second. Nope, you head straight for the soda, pour some and take a swig. Ahhhh! So much for breakfast!

In case you're wondering, this is not a nutritious breakfast choice! Any girl who wants to look her best should know this: Eating a balanced diet is the best beauty trick in the book!

But if this picture rings a bell for you, then you also share something else with most teens: poor eating habits. It's true. Today's teens and pre-teens eat worse than any other age group in the country!

That's bad news because now is the time you need good nutrition most! That way, when you're older, you'll already have established good eating habits. Why else, you ask? You can probably figure it out yourself. If you haven't already noticed, you soon will: The pre-teen and teen years are when your body does most of its growing. Also, as your body grows, its shape changes. Boys and girls begin to look less and less alike. Maybe that's one of the reasons that boys and girls start noticing each other at about this same time!

BODY BASICS

Before puberty, boys and girls are more or less evenly matched in terms of body composition. But with puberty's onset, much of that changes. Male and female bodies begin producing different chemicals called hormones. Boys' bodies make testosterone and girls' bodies make estrogen. What happens, as a result, is that a girl's body fat increases—sometimes by as much as forty pounds or so during her teens. She develops breasts and her pelvis and hips widen. Boys, on the other hand, gain only about half as much body fat. Instead, they develop more muscle tissue and grow taller.

Because you are in your fastest-growing years, it's crucial that you eat the healthy foods that will keep up with and encourage that growth. In the same way that a plant won't grow if it doesn't get enough water and sunlight, your body can't grow strong, beautiful, and healthy if it doesn't get enough of the building materials it needs. Oops! That probably sounds 'ike one of those things your parents tell you when you're sitting at the dinner table and your lima beans are still on your plate. You can almost hear them say: "If you don't eat your vegetables . . . !" Ugh!

5

Your parents may not even know exactly *why* it's important for you to eat well. If they did, they'd bug you even more about it! Here are a couple of good reasons:

Poor nutrition may delay the arrival of your maturation process. Believe it or not, it can even prevent you from reaching your full growth potential. You don't want to be smaller than you should be, do you? Not a good idea for girls who hope to play basketball or be fashion models! And yet, for most young women, nutrition still takes a backseat to almost everything else in their lives!

Something else happens when girls start to reach puberty. Lots of them don't know what to make of their sudden growth spurts. They see their hips getting curvy and their breasts appearing, and often

Pineapples alone will <u>not</u> make you thinner . . .

. . . And neither will these.

think: FAT! What too many girls may not realize is that this is all part of the puberty plan. They don't quite know what to make of their new "additions." Next step? They try to control their weight—and you know what that means: a DIET!

It's been estimated that thirty to sixty percent of girls in their teens are dieting—whether they're overweight or not! You've probably heard of some of the more outrageous ones, like the "Ice Cream Diet" or the "Pineapple Diet." All claim to have some kind of magic that will make you thin! The problem is, most teenage girls don't know that at the same time they're cutting down on calories, they may be cutting out some of those much-needed nutrients their growing bodies beg for. Whatever you do, stay away from fad diets; they're not the answer. Worse, they may even do serious damage to your health.

WHAT DO YOU KNOW?

Before we get down to the nitty gritty, let's find out how much you *really* know about nutrition. Hint: To help you out, some of the questions are drawn from what you've read here so far.

For all quizzes, please write your answers on a separate sheet of paper.

☆☆ EATING PRETTY QUIZ ☆☆

1. *There's nothing nutritious about a ''burger-fries-and-a-shake'' meal.*
   True or False
2. *If your parents are overweight, that means you will be, too.*
   True or False
3. *All kinds of foods that contain fat are bad for you.*
   True or False
4. *It's better to skip a meal than to eat something at a fast-food restaurant.*
   True or False
5. *What I eat has very little effect on how I look.*
   True or False
6. *Because girls gain more fat tissue during puberty, they shouldn't eat as much.*
   True or False
7. *Even if you think you eat a well-balanced diet, it's a good idea to take a daily multivitamin supplement.*
   True or False

Answers: 1. False 2. False 3. False 4. False 5. False 6. False 7. True

8

☆☆☆

If you're surprised to learn that only statement number 7 is true, then it might not be a bad idea to read on to find out WHY! Hmmmm. Seems there's more to nutrition than meets the eye, after all!

If someone promised you there was a magic potion that could make you look and feel better, you'd probably want to know where you could get it. Unfortunately, there's no such thing. There isn't even one "super-food"—though Popeye claimed spinach was his—that can turn you into a wonder woman.

Maybe you're one of those people who's convinced that she'll always be a Junk-Food Jane. Still, if you've paid careful attention to what you've read so far, you have to admit that there are lots of good reasons to at least explore more about Eating Pretty and what it can do for you. With a little luck, you may even decide that eating good food makes you feel so good that you'll never eat poorly again!

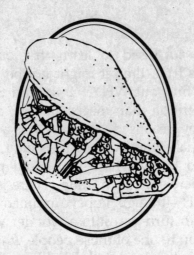

Balance — for a Better You!

You hear it all the time: The food you want to eat, such as the sweet roll for breakfast, *isn't* good for you, but the lima beans that you'd prefer to leave on your plate *are* good for you! Is there any food out there that is both delicious and nutritious? The answer is— YES! And the aim of this book is to help you find those foods so you can enjoy healthy eating.

Before you can begin to make healthy eating a habit, it helps to know more about the food that you put into your mouth. All food is made up of various parts called nutrients. There are five different kinds of nutrients: **proteins, carbohydrates, fats, vitamins and min-**

10

erals. Each nutrient has its own "job," and they all rely on each other to work properly. You might think of them as a kind of sports team, whose combined goal is to keep your body going strong. And although it is not a nutrient, water is a very important player on this team as you will read later in this chapter.

Proteins, carbohydrates and fats are the three key players of the nutrient team. Together, they provide your body with energy in the form of—you guessed it—calories.

PROTEINS: YOUR BODY'S BUILDING BLOCKS

Protein is an especially important nutrient for young, growing bodies like yours. Protein helps "build your body" by building new tissues like those in your bones, muscles, skin and hair, and repairing old ones. And your body uses protein to make antibodies—your body's first line of defense against infection. Protein also helps ensure that both nutrients and oxygen get to where they're supposed to go in your body.

If you were to take a microscopic look at protein, you would see that it contains things called *amino acids*. Your resourceful body produces most of these amino acids on its own, but some—the essential amino acids—you can get only from certain foods. If you go long enough without them, you're asking for trouble with a capital "T." To avoid this, you need to eat enough protein on a *daily* basis.

WHERE CAN YOU GET 'EM?

These foods earn the title of *complete* proteins. This simply means that by eating them, you'll get the amino acids you need.

- Meat: beef, liver, lamb (Note: red meat tends to be high in fat, so try to limit your intake to two servings a week.)
- Poultry: chicken, turkey
- Fish, including shellfish
- Eggs
- Milk and milk products, such as cheese and yogurt

Nuts, seeds, grains, and vegetables called "legumes" also provide protein, but because they're missing some of the amino acids you need, they only get to be called *incomplete* proteins. So, while eating a bagful of sunflower seeds may be fun and delicious, you're packing away only a portion of the protein power you need. Sunflower seeds are a good snack, but they can't be substituted for complete proteins.

Ideally, about fifteen percent of your calories should come from protein.

CARBOHYDRATES: THE ENERGY ESSENTIALS

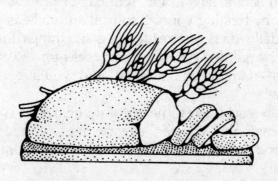

Like most young people, you're probably full of "get-up-and-go." No matter what age you happen to be, though, carbohydrates give your body the energy it needs to do all the wonderful things it does. Whether you're studying for a spelling quiz, shopping with your friends, or even sleeping comfortably at night, carbohydrates help keep your bodily functions functioning.

WHERE CAN YOU GET 'EM?

There are basically two kinds of carbohydrates: *simple carbohydrates*, better known as sugar, and *complex carbohydrates*, better known as starch. Lots of girls are all too familiar with simple carbohydrates—and you probably get more than your share. Any time you gobble up something sweet—cookies, cake, or most breakfast cereals—it's likely that you're consuming a fair amount of the stuff in the form of refined sugar. Too much refined sugar isn't good for you.

There are some good-for-you foods, like fruit and milk, that are also simple carbohydrates—meaning they also contain sugar. The difference? These foods contain *natural* sugar, not "refined" or processed sugar. So, by treating yourself to fruit and milk as part of your daily diet, you're doing good things for your body by getting vitamins and calcium. Reach for sweets—natural fruit sweets—and you'll be eating healthy!

When you choose the natural sugar and complex carbs over the sweeter, sugary ones, you're doing your body a big favor. The simple carbohydrates do give the body a quick energy fix—they're rapidly absorbed into the bloodstream—but they do little else than provide you with calories. In fact, this is one of the biggest differences between simple and complex carbohydrates: The former are usually loaded with calories; the latter are not.

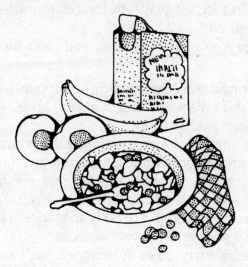

A complete breakfast provides lots of complex carbohydrates.

Complex carbohydrates, or starches, include:
- Breads, cereals, grains
- Pasta
- Potatoes
- Vegetables

Ideally, about fifty-five to sixty percent of your calories should come from carbohydrates.

FATS: YOU CAN'T JUST FORGET 'EM

In the same way that we need a certain amount of both proteins and carbohydrates in our diet, we also need fat. In fact, fat plays an important part—a vital part—in our diet.

Here are a few other reasons you can't just forget about fat:

- Fat is necessary for growth; it supplies your tissues and cells with "essential fatty acids"—which they can't do without.
- Fat is our most concentrated food source. Proteins and carbohydrates contain four calories per gram, while fat has almost nine calories per gram—more than double the energy.
- Fat can be stored in the body to give us a back-up energy supply when we need it.
- Fat helps carry other substances, such as certain vitamins, through your bloodstream so they can get to the cells where they'll be used.
- Fat acts as a cushion for your organs.
- The fat under your skin serves as insulation against hot and cold temperatures.
- Fat helps put your hunger pangs to rest by making you feel full.

As you can see, fat serves several important functions. Fat also makes food taste good, which is the reason that, unfortunately, most people in our country tend to eat lots more fat than their bodies actually need. Believe it or not, the average American's diet

16

contains about forty percent fat. How much of your diet should come from fat? No more than thirty percent.

Many studies have shown that young people, in particular, eat too many fatty foods. How *much* fat your diet contains is only half the issue, though. If you really want to eat healthy, then you've also got to be aware of what *kind* of fat you're eating. All fats are not alike.

Fat comes in different forms—*saturated* and *unsaturated* fats. If you forget which fats are which, just remember this easy test: A saturated fat will usually become solid at room temperature—think of bacon grease—and practically always hardens in the fridge. Saturated fats are the ones you've got to watch out for. Too much of them now can mean mega-health problems later.

SATURATED FATS

Found in these foods:

- Beef
- Poultry
- Milk
- Butter
- Cheese
- Egg yolks
- Vegetable shortening
- Partially and/or hydrogenated vegetable oils
- The "tropical" oils—coconut oil, palm and palm kernel oil

And some not-so-sweet news for chocoholics: Chocolate is one more place you'll find saturated fat.

Young women need to eat a balanced diet that contains fatty foods, but low-fat choices are best. Don't eat beef for dinner every night, but two or three times a week is fine. Don't limit your poultry intake. Instead of whole milk, drink low-fat milk. Instead of butter, use margarine. Instead of cheddar cheese, choose mozzarella. At your age, eggs are a good choice, just not every day.

Unsaturated fats can be broken down into two smaller groups: the *monounsaturated* and *polyunsaturated* fats. For our purposes here, let's focus on the polyunsaturated fats.

On your next trip to the grocery store, check out all the different types of oil on the shelf. You'll find corn oil, safflower oil and sunflower oil, to name a few. They may have different names, but all are sources of polyunsaturated fats.

POLYUNSATURATED FATS

Found in these foods:

- ✪ Fish
- ✪ Margarine
- ✪ Corn oil
- ✪ Safflower oil
- ✪ Sunflower oil
- ✪ Cottonseed oil
- ✪ Soybean oil

So what's the big deal about polyunsaturated fats? Well, they just may be the good guys in Fat City. Evidence shows that small doses of these fats actually help keep that sinister culprit, *cholesterol*, from building up in your blood.

Saturated fats, however, do just the opposite—and have been linked to higher cholesterol levels. Your best bet, of course, is to limit your fat intake as much as possible. When you've got to have it, go for the polyunsaturated stuff.

Another fat fact: You know that french fries are fried in oil—fat. But some fat is sneaky and you may not be able to see the fat in foods such as donuts, potato chips, ice cream, etc. It's there! Start reading labels to be on the safe side. BEWARE! Too much fat is bad news for your body.

THE FABULOUS FOUR: FOOD GROUPS TO GROW ON

Simply put, a balanced diet is one that includes all the nutrients you need in the proper amounts. *Hmmmm*, you're thinking. The *"proper amount"*? Don't worry; you don't have to add up grams and calories all day—unless you want to. To look and feel your best, growing girls like you need to eat:

VOILÀ! THE FAB FOUR!

✪ **Meat Group:** *Lean meat, fish, poultry, eggs, legumes, cheese, dried beans*—TWO TO THREE SERVINGS A DAY.

✪ **Vegetable and Fruit Group:** *All kinds*—FOUR SERVINGS A DAY.

✪ **Milk Group:** *Low-fat or skim milk, cheese, yogurt, ice cream*—FOUR SERVINGS A DAY.

✪ **Bread and Cereal Groups:** *Cereals, breads, rice, pasta*—FOUR SERVINGS A DAY.

Why eat a balanced diet? Consider this: Including vitamins and minerals, there are more than fifty nutrients your body needs to blossom. Since no one has discovered one food that "has it all," the only way to get all fifty-plus is to eat a balanced diet that includes a variety of foods.

DON'T FORGET ABOUT THE OTHERS!

In this age of fast food and microwave ovens, it's quite difficult to eat everything you should every day. A missed breakfast here, a skipped lunch there. . . . But remember, vitamins and minerals are members of your "nutrient team," too. It's best to get them from the foods you eat, but some doctors recommend taking vitamin supplements to make up for what you may be missing. **Ask your mom or your doctor about taking vitamins**.

There are two types of vitamins—*fat soluble* and *water soluble*. Fat-soluble vitamins can be stored in your body for later use; it is not necessary for you to consume them daily. Water-soluble vitamins are absorbed through the intestines, then flushed out of the body if not used. There are nine water-soluble vitamins, including vitamin C; six are listed in the chart on the following pages.

VITAMINS

Fruits and vegetables are great sources of vitamins and minerals.

FAT-SOLUBLE VITAMINS

Vitamin A
What it helps: Vision, skin, teeth, tissue growth/repair.

Which foods contain it: Dark green and yellow veggies, cantaloupe, eggs, liver.

Vitamin D
What it helps: Calcium absorption for teeth and bones.

Which foods contain it: Milk, eggs, butter, salmon, tuna.

Vitamin E
What it helps: Aids in production of red blood cells, muscles and other tissues.

Which foods contain it: Vegetable oils, dried beans, margarine, whole-grain breads and cereals.

Vitamin K
What it helps: Blood clotting, metabolism.

Which foods contain it: Pork, beef, dark green leafy vegetables, cauliflower, tomatoes, peas and carrots.

WATER-SOLUBLE VITAMINS

Vitamin B_1 (Thiamine)
What it helps: Releases energy from carbohydrates, growth/repair of tissues, maintains health of heart, nervous system, muscles and intestines.

Which foods contain it: Lean pork, eggs, whole-grain breads and cereals, green vegetables, plums, prunes and raisins.

Vitamin B_2 (Riboflavin)
What it helps: Skin, body's use of oxygen.

Which foods contain it: Dark green leafy vegetables, broccoli, lean meat, eggs and all dairy products, salmon, whole-grain breads and cereals.

Vitamin B_3 (Niacin)
What it helps: See B_1 and B_2.

Which foods contain it: See B_1 and B_2.

Vitamin B$_6$ (Pyridoxine)
What it helps: Absorption of protein, resistance to stress.

Which foods contain it: Fish, poultry, peanuts, spinach, bananas, yams, whole-grain breads and cereals.

Vitamin B$_{12}$ (Cobalamin)
What it helps: Protein, fat and carbohydrate metabolism, aids in production of red blood cells.

Which foods contain it: Lean meat, eggs, fish, milk and milk products.

Vitamin C (Ascorbic Acid)
What it helps: Formation/strengthening of bones and teeth.

Which foods contain it: Green peppers, broccoli and other green veggies are best sources; also, citrus fruits, cantaloupe, strawberries, tomatoes and potatoes.

MAGIC MINERALS

Like vitamins, minerals—all sixteen of them—have specific functions. Calcium and iron are two minerals that many young people don't get enough of. You need calcium for strong bones and teeth, so don't skimp on calcium-rich foods such as milk, cheese, broccoli and spinach. Get your fill of iron by eating more liver (just try!), shellfish (scallops, shrimp and clams), lean hamburger—even sunflower seeds and watermelon.

WATER, WATER, EVERYWHERE

Would you believe that about two-thirds of your body is made up of water? Your blood is full of water. Your muscles (seventy-five percent water) and bones (twenty-two percent water) also have a good dose of the wet stuff. Actually, you've got water everywhere. If you had to you could live for a while—maybe even several weeks—without food. Water is another story. A few days without water, and you're all washed up!

Wonderful water carries nutrients to your blood. It is vital for digestion, waste elimination and helping your body to keep its cool—that's why you perspire. It also acts as a lubricant for your muscles and joints.

Most of the foods you eat, especially fruits and vegetables, contain water, as do milk, juices and other liquids. Still, you should try to drink lots of water every day—eight glasses if you can—to keep things flowing smoothly in your system.

LOW IN CALORIES, HIGH IN FAT? A LESSON IN LABEL READING

A simple trip to the supermarket can sabotage your healthy eating plans—unless you take the time to become "label literate." It's really easier than you think. Actually, most of what's on the label is stuff you've already learned in this chapter. Best of all, once you know what to look for, you'll no longer be fooled by the slick packaging many food companies use to sell their products.

Let's look at a can of basic broccoli soup to get an idea:

BROCCOLI SOUP

Nutrition Information Per Serving
Serving Size   4 oz. (8 oz. prepared)
Servings per container   2 and ¾
Calories   140
Protein   5 grams
Total Carbohydrates   15 grams
Simple sugars   6 grams
Complex carbohydrates   9 grams
Fat   7 grams
Sodium   720 mg./serving
Percentage of U.S. Recommended Daily Allowances (RDA):
Protein   10
Vitamin A   10
Vitamin C   15
Thiamine   4
Riboflavin   10
Niacin   2
Calcium   10
Iron   4

Ingredients: Chicken broth, broccoli, wheat flour, cream, onion, water, butter, cornstarch, salt, sugar, natural flavoring and spice.

Ingredients are listed in order of the amount used, i.e. the dominant ingredient listed first. In addition, perishable foods—milk, orange juice, yogurt, etc.— also include a *date* that tells you how long the food will be fresh.

In addition to the expiration date, the one tidbit of information you should make a habit of checking on *all* foods is the fat content. Many microwave meals contain fewer than 300 calories. But what these low-cal meals don't point out as plainly is the amount of fat they have. (Many are also high in sodium.) Here's how to calculate how many of those calories come from fat:

HOW MUCH FAT DO YOU EAT?

Let the label be your guide.

Let's turn back to the label on the soup can and find out how much fat is in the soup. Here's how to do it:

---

1. Find the grams of fat per serving listed on the label.
2. Multiply this number by 9 to determine the number of calories from fat. Why 9? There are 9 calories in each gram of fat.
3. Use this formula to find the % of calories from fat:

$$\frac{(\text{grams of fat per serving} \times 9)}{(\text{total calories per serving})} \times 100$$

Here's an example using the soup can label:

$$\frac{7 \times 9}{140} = \frac{63 \text{ total calories}}{140 \text{ total calories}} = .45 \times 100 = 45\%$$

Remember, no more than thirty percent of your daily calories should come from fat. If this seems a bit complicated to do in your head, you might want to carry a mini-calculator with you when you shop. After a while, you'll become such a label pro that everyone will be coming to you for label lessons.

ADDITIVES & PRESERVATIVES: EXTRAS EXCESS?

WHAT'S ALL THIS FUSS ABOUT "FRESH"?

Lots of people insist on eating only fresh and natural (unprocessed) foods. Vegetables or fruits from a can? Frozen dinners? Spaghetti sauce in a jar? Ha! Not for these people. Hmmm. Maybe it's time to ask, "Why?"

Take a closer look at the labels on some of these prepackaged foods. Read the very end of the ingredient list. What do you see? Probably a few words with impossible-to-pronounce names. Most of these are chemicals. For example, a popular brand of salsa (sauce commonly used in Mexican food) includes something called "benzoate of soda." Any guesses as to what it's doing in the salsa, along with the tomatoes, water, chilies, tomato paste, vinegar, garlic and salt?

Benzoate of soda is added to the salsa to help preserve it—to keep it fresh. It is, therefore, an additive which acts as a preservative. There are thousands of different additives—and they do a number of different jobs. Preservatives, obviously, preserve. Antioxidants also help prevent food from spoiling. Emulsifiers help foods freeze better. Artificial dyes enhance the color of food. One additive you may have heard about is MSG, or monosodium glutamate, often used to enhance the flavor of foods.

Most additives that go into your foods are added for a good reason (e.g. so your crackers won't turn moldy on your shelf). In fact, all chemicals go through extensive testing before the Food and Drug Administration will approve them to be added to foods. Many people remain convinced that some of these chemicals may not be good for your health. For instance, many people report that they feel ill after eating foods containing MSG. As with any food or chemical, some people may react negatively and need to avoid eating that food or chemical.

Your best bet yet, is to stick to fresh food and avoid any possible problems. Making spaghetti sauce from scratch definitely takes longer than opening a can, but if you can avoid these chemicals, you are probably eating healthier.

"HEALTH" FOODS: HEALTHIER OR JUST A LOT OF HYPE?

The aisles of a "health food" store don't look like those you see in a typical grocery store. They're stocked with many foods that some people claim are extra-healthy for you. Are they? That depends. Carob chips aren't much better for you than chocolate chips. Molasses is just another form of sugar.

Health food stores aren't always good nutritional bets. Besides being very expensive, many health food products can be sky-high in sugar and fat. And many "diet" foods aren't low in calories because they are made for diabetics, and thus contain another type of sweetener (sorbitol) which is even higher in calories than refined sugar.

On the other hand, health food stores do make a point of carrying some products that you may not always find at regular markets. Among them: "organically grown," pesticide-free vegetables; and chickens that were raised in smaller numbers, so they didn't need to be fed mass doses of antibiotics. These products are usually more expensive, but many people feel that they are much safer to eat, and worth the extra cost.

28

What about products such as "protein powders" and energy-boosting supplements? Some people swear by them; others think they're a bunch of hogwash.

Caution: Always check with a doctor or registered dietician before trying something you don't know anything about. Besides, a well-balanced diet should give you all the energy you need.

☆☆ FOOD-MATCHING QUIZ ☆☆

Try to put the following foods in their appropriate nutrient group:

(C) Carbohydrate, (F) Fat, or (P) Protein.

1. *Fish*	6. *Spaghetti*	11. *Mayonnaise*
2. *Butter*	7. *Hamburger*	12. *Potato*
3. *Bagel*	8. *Egg*	13. *Pasta*
4. *Orange*	9. *Strawberry*	14. *Chicken*
5. *Broccoli*	10. *Cookie*	

Answers: 1. P; 2. F; 3. C; 4. C; 5. C; 6. C; 7. P; 8. P; 9. C; 10. C; 11. F; 12. C; 13. C; 14. P

☆☆☆

Why French Fries are Favorites and Liver Gets Left on Your Plate

Why do you eat what you eat? Ever ask yourself that question? Actually, many factors influence your eating habits: your family, friends—even the media. It's a process that starts before you even have any say in the matter—when you're still sputtering baby talk.

The foods parents feed their young children often affect the food choices those same kids will make when they're older. Now, this doesn't mean that you can blame your sweet tooth on your mom. Still, when you're young, Mom or Dad is the main menu-planner. As you've grown older (and sneakier), you may have learned the fine art of basket-stuffing: Your mom turns her back for a moment, and, as if by magic, your favorite sugar-coated cereal, cookies and soft drinks find their way into her shopping cart.

Hey, wait a minute. You're reading this book because you want to learn more about nutrition, right? Luckily, your food choices are influenced by these external factors only as much as you let them be. Who knows? You may decide it's time to stop basket-stuffing and "talk turkey" about nutrition with your folks.

HOW YOU LIVE AFFECTS WHAT YOU EAT, TOO

Some people decide early on that they want to be vegetarians. Others use food to make a statement about their personal beliefs. Even your religion can make a difference in what you eat or don't eat.

WHAT TICKLES *YOUR* TASTE BUDS?

You have your own personal taste in music, in clothes, in people. Why shouldn't you prefer certain foods? One reason so many people can't stick to a diet

31

is that they're told to eat certain foods—many of which they don't like. Would you stay on such a diet? Probably not.

"WHAT-ARE-YOU-EATING?" CHART

Keep track of what you eat for an entire week to find out more about your own food preferences and eating habits. It's easy. In a notebook write the following headings on a page:
- ❂ DATE AND TIME I'M EATING
- ❂ WHAT AND HOW MUCH I ATE
- ❂ WHO WAS WITH ME
- ❂ WHERE I WAS EATING
- ❂ WHAT I WAS THINKING ABOUT

Allow one page for each day of the week. Make sure you keep track of everything you *eat* and *drink*. Also, don't just write, "snack—peanuts." Include how many peanuts you ate. Once you get the hang of it, you might even discover that taking nutrition notes can even be FUN. Enjoy!

Perhaps you're a member of your school's swim team, and have to wake up early for workouts. The last thing you have time for is breakfast. It's tough enough just waking up before the sun rises. But as an athlete, your body could benefit from the extra energy.

Maybe you're a gal on the go who's got more extra-curricular activities than pairs of socks: after-school meetings, drama club, cheerleading, or band. With such a hectic schedule, you often forget to make time to eat.

On the other hand, you might be more sedentary, and love nothing more than plopping in front of the tube (potato chip bag in hand) after a hard day at school.

You can easily see how your living habits and your eating habits go hand in hand. The end result, unfortunately, is that together they often work against you. If you aren't careful, they can wreak havoc with your nutritional needs.

MICROWAVE MAGIC

Today, what and when families eat is often a matter of what's convenient. We eat out more. We call for Chinese take-out and pizza. Thanks to microwaves, almost anyone can just push a button, and—ZAP!—dinner is ready in an instant.

Unfortunately, many young people fall into this kind of eat-on-the-run lifestyle. If you really want to make healthy eating a habit, you'll have to make some changes. You'll need to spend some time *planning* what you eat. Not hours of slaving in the kitchen—just a little know-how, a bit of preparation, and you're set. This easy "get-you-through-the-week" menu is a good place to start.

SERVING SIZES

When you're planning your own daily menu, let the Basic Four Food Groups be your guide. Check the list below so you'll know exactly how much of a particular food equals "one serving."

Milk Group: (4 servings a day)

1 cup milk, yogurt
1 cup cottage cheese
1½ ounces cheese
1¾ cups ice cream (choose ice milk or frozen yogurt as a
   low-fat alternative)
1 cup pudding

Meat Group: (2-3 servings totaling 8-9 ounces of protein daily)

4 ounces meat, fish, poultry
2 eggs
1 cup dried beans, peas
2 tablespoons peanut butter

Vegetable and Fruit Group: (4 servings a day)

1 cup raw vegetables
½ cup cooked vegetables
1 medium-sized piece of fruit (1 orange, apple, etc.)
½ cup fruit or vegetable juice

Bread and Cereal Group: (4 servings a day)

1 slice bread
1 cup cold cereal
½ cup cooked cereal (oatmeal, etc.)
½ cup cooked pasta

EATING PRETTY MENUS

To feel good and look great, we suggest using these
sample menus as your guide to *Eating Pretty*. Start the
day with a burst of energy. Choose a lunch designed
to keep you going, and help plan nutritious and delicious family dinners. Mom will be thrilled by your
help in the kitchen, too!

A "GET-UP-AND-GO" BREAKFAST

MONDAY
Orange
Whole-grain toast (optional: jelly and/or margarine)
Low-fat or skim milk
Egg (any style, your choice)

TUESDAY
Mixed berries (strawberries, blueberries, etc.)
Cereal (go for the low- or no-sugar healthy ones)
Low-fat or skim milk for cereal

WEDNESDAY
½ grapefruit (Sprinkle on a dash of cinnamon!)
French toast made with whole-wheat bread, with pure maple
  syrup
Low-fat fruit yogurt

THURSDAY
Apple juice
Raisin-bran muffin
Low-fat cottage cheese with fresh fruit

FRIDAY
Cantaloupe wedge with low-fat yogurt
Hot cereal (such as oatmeal—add raisins for a sweet taste)
Low-fat or skim milk (for hot cereal)

QUICK-ENERGY LUNCH:
BEST BETS FOR BROWN-BAGGIN' IT

MONDAY
Cold leftover chicken (breast or leg)
Celery sticks
Banana-oatmeal cookies*
Low-fat or skim milk

TUESDAY
Peanut butter and banana sandwich on raisin bread
Orange
Low-fat or skim milk

35

WEDNESDAY
Tuna fish salad in a pita pocket (with lettuce and tomato)
Cucumber wedges
Apple
Low-fat or skim milk

THURSDAY
Turkey breast sandwich on whole-wheat bread
Carrot sticks
Peanut butter balls*
Low-fat or skim milk

FRIDAY
Egg salad sandwich on English muffin
Cherry tomatoes, carrot and zucchini sticks—take along some
    homemade spinach dip* to go with 'em.
Oatmeal cookies
Low-fat or skim milk

DELICIOUS DINNERS

MONDAY
Lean pork chop
Baked potato (optional: margarine or yogurt)
Steamed broccoli
Fresh pineapple
Low-fat or skim milk

TUESDAY
Fresh spinach and lettuce salad (dressing on side used spar-
    ingly)
Roasted turkey
Cornbread
Sugar-free pudding
Low-fat or skim milk

WEDNESDAY
Fish 1-2-3*
Pasta (as side dish)
The Greatest Green Beans*
Low-fat or skim milk

THURSDAY
Tossed green salad
Spaghetti with (lean) meatballs

Steamed zucchini
Mixed fruit salad
Low-fat or skim milk

FRIDAY
Crispy Baked Chicken*
Far-East Vegetables*
Brown rice
Mandarin oranges
Low-fat or skim milk

HEALTHY, HEARTY SNACKS

MONDAY
Peach Milkshake*
Wheat crackers

TUESDAY
Banana-Strawberry Smoothie*

WEDNESDAY
Pear-Oatmeal Muffin*

THURSDAY
Tortilla with melted part-skim mozzarella cheese

FRIDAY
Dry-roasted mixed nuts
Orange juice

*You'll find these recipes in our EATING PRETTY RECIPES sections later in the book.

Your new-found enthusiasm for good-for-you foods might just encourage some creative cooking. If you've stayed out of the kitchen until now, or are someone who usually turns toast into a blackened, cardboard-like creation, have no fear! Cooking, once you know the basics, is probably a lot easier than some of your homework. So, step right up. Before you know it, you'll be serving it up like a chef supreme.

COMMON SENSE AND SAFETY
IN THE KITCHEN

Before you get ready to cook up a storm, make sure to read this section on simple-but-important safety practices in the kitchen. A safe kitchen is a happy kitchen!

1. **Always** get your mom's or dad's (or older sibling's) permission and, more important, their *help and supervision*, before you start cooking in the kitchen.

2. Keep a box of baking soda handy. It's great for putting out small kitchen fires. (Tip: A box in the refrigerator really does help to kill food odors.)

3. Take care when cutting! Never cut *toward* your body, but always *away* from it. Keep your fingers tucked under while chopping, dicing, slicing, shredding, etc. Always use a vegetable peeler (not a knife) for peeling both fruits and vegetables.

4. Don't forget to turn off the stove, or to unplug electrical appliances when you're done with them.

5. **Never, ever** stick your fingers OR a utensil (such as a spoon) into a mixer, blender, garbage disposal, etc.

6. When you're cooking on a stove, make sure that handles aren't left sticking out over the stove's edge. Otherwise, it's possible for little kids to get at them, or someone else—including you—might accidentally bump into them and get burned.

7. Electrical appliances should *never* be used on a wet countertop, nor with wet hands. These same appliances should *never* be placed in the sink. When cleaning, make sure the cord is unplugged, and even then avoid getting the connection site wet.

8. **Don't ever** use a utensil or other metal object to pry something loose from appliances like toasters. You could be electrocuted!
9. Metal, including aluminum foil, is strictly off-limits in the microwave.

SAFETY TIPS REGARDING FOOD

1. Always check freshness and/or expiration dates of all ingredients before adding them to your recipe. For example, before putting eggs into a batter mix, crack each one into a small cup. If the egg seems okay (has no odor), then add it to the rest of the ingredients.
2. Always wash fruits and vegetables in warm, soapy water for two to three minutes, then rinse thoroughly in cold water before eating or cooking. Lots of produce comes straight from the grocery store still "wearing" unhealthy pesticides.

EATING PRETTY RECIPES

Just because you're eating healthy now, you don't have to do without terrific, yummy-in-the-tummy foods. You'll find that the recipes below combine good taste with good health. So, happy cooking—and happy eating.

In some of the following recipes, you'll see the words "light" or "low-fat." This simply means that the product—mayonnaise, salad dressing, etc.—

contains less oil or fat. We do *not* recommend using so-called "diet" products, which often contain more additives and preservatives. These chemicals are not part of our healthy eating plan.

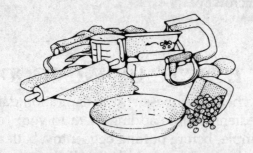

POWER-PACKED PARTY SNACKS

SPINACH DIP*

1 (10 oz.) pkg. frozen chopped spinach, thawed
1½ cups low-fat cottage cheese
½ cup low-fat or skim milk
½ cup light mayonnaise
1 Tbs. lemon juice
½ tsp. onion powder
¼ tsp. garlic powder
1 tsp. herb seasoning
½ tsp. pepper
1 Tbs. dill weed

Drain spinach and squeeze out excess moisture. Combine remaining ingredients in a blender or food processor and blend until smooth and creamy. Mix in spinach. Chill. Serve with raw vegetables and/or crackers. *Makes 4 cups.*

TASTY STUFFED MUSHROOMS*

½ lb. whole, fresh mushrooms
¼ cup Parmesan cheese
¼ cup bread crumbs
¼ tsp. basil

¼ **tsp. oregano**
⅛ **tsp. thyme**

Wash mushrooms and separate the stems from the caps. Combine the cheese, bread crumbs, basil, oregano, thyme and mushroom stems in a food processor or blender and purée. Spoon the mixture into the mushroom caps. Bake at 425 degrees for 5 minutes or until the mushrooms are tender. *Makes 6 servings.*

MINI-PIZZAS*

1 pkg. of 4 whole-wheat English muffins
1 small can pizza sauce (or tomato sauce)
¾ to 1 cup grated cheese (combine cheddar and mozzarella for less fat)

Slice English muffins in half. Spread with pizza sauce. Sprinkle with cheese. Bake about 10 minutes in a 450 degree oven. Option: Add veggies, such as onions, fresh tomato, olives or green pepper on top before baking. *Serves 4.*

BANANA POPS*

4 bananas, peeled
Milk
8 wooden popsicle sticks
1 cup peanut butter
1 Tbs. vegetable shortening
Chopped nuts (optional)
Shredded coconut (optional)

Cut bananas in half, crosswise. Insert wooden stick in end of each and freeze. Melt peanut butter in a double boiler[†] over hot water, stir in shortening and, if needed, add a little milk until peanut butter is runny. Coat each frozen banana half with the peanut butter mixture, and roll immediately in nuts or coconut if desired. Eat now or refreeze. *Makes 8 pops.*

[†](A double boiler is two pans stacked together. The lower pan holds water, which surrounds the upper pan. The water heats up and gently cooks the contents of the upper pan. Ask your mom if she has a double boiler. If she doesn't, ask her to show you how to make one by filling a large saucepan with water, and putting a smaller pan inside it so the lower part of

the smaller pan is in the water. Then add the peanut butter to the smaller pan, cover and cook gently. **MAKE SURE TO HAVE YOUR MOM'S HELP WHEN COOKING WITH A DOUBLE BOILER.**)

MARVELOUS MAIN DISHES

Who says YOU can't make a healthy dinner for the entire family? Just wait until you try these easy palate-pleasers.

CRISPY BAKED CHICKEN*

1 chicken fryer (2-3 pounds), cut up, (you can buy it this way
   at the grocery store), skin and fat removed
½ tsp. paprika
½ tsp. pepper
1 cup low-fat or skim milk
1 cup cornflake crumbs

Sprinkle chicken pieces with paprika and pepper. Dip in milk and roll in crumbs. Place in a baking dish sprayed with non-stick spray. Be sure that the pieces don't touch. Bake for 45 minutes or until tender in a 400 degree oven. *Makes 4 servings.*

FISH 1-2-3

1 whitefish, turbot or halibut filet
Light mayonnaise
Sweet onions, thinly sliced
Dill weed
Parsley

Preheat oven to 350 degrees. Rinse fish and pat dry on paper towel. Use a 9" × 13" Pyrex dish and spray with nonstick cooking spray. Line with thinly sliced onions. "Paint" the fish on both sides with mayonnaise. Place fish on top of onions and sprinkle with dill and a little parsley. Bake at 350 degrees for 30 minutes. *Serves 1.*

STUFFED TUNA ROLLS

1 can tuna, packed in water
¼ cup grated cheddar cheese
¼ cup grated mozzarella cheese
1 Tbs. minced onion

2 Tbs. chili sauce
2 Tbs. relish
2 Tbs. light mayonnaise
1 Tbs. lemon juice
2 large whole-wheat rolls

Drain tuna and flake into a bowl. Combine all ingredients except the rolls in the same bowl. Stir until blended. Slice 1 inch off one end of each roll. Scoop out center and discard. Spoon tuna mixture into rolls. Wrap in foil. Bake 30 minutes in 350 degree oven. May be served hot or cold. *Serves 2.*

LEMON-TARRAGON CHICKEN

2 whole chicken breasts, halved and skinned
¼ cup apple juice
2 Tbs. lemon juice
2 tsp. vegetable oil
¼-½ tsp. minced, peeled garlic
2 tsp. dried tarragon leaves
¼ tsp. pepper

Rinse chicken and pat dry. Combine remaining ingredients in 12″ × 9″ × 2″ baking dish. Place chicken in dish and turn chicken to coat thoroughly. Cover and chill 2-4 hours. Bake uncovered for 1 hour at 350 degrees, basting with pan juices every 10 minutes during last 30 minutes. If desired, place under broiler at the last minute for 2-3 minutes or until brown. Serve chicken with pan juices. *Serves 4.*

VERY-EASY VEGGIES

You get the most nutrients from vegetables that are either raw or steamed. Every once in a while, though, you might get a craving for a new veggie variation—and these fit the bill.

THE GREATEST GREEN BEANS

16 oz. (2 cups) fresh green beans (with ends snapped off)
½ lb. *lean* ground beef
½ small onion, minced
1 (8 oz.) can tomato juice

Brown meat and onions. Drain off fat. Add beans. Mix well with tomato juice. Simmer for 30 minutes on low heat. *Serves 4.*

GLAZED PARSLEY CARROTS*

1¼ lbs. peeled and sliced carrots (4 cups)
Ground pepper
½ tsp. sugar
¼ cup water
1 Tbs. lemon juice
2 Tbs. margarine
2 Tbs. finely chopped parsley

Place carrots in saucepan. Add pepper, sugar, water, lemon juice and margarine. Cover and cook over moderately high heat, shaking pan occasionally. Cook about 7 minutes until carrots are tender, the liquid has evaporated, and the carrots are lightly glazed. Take care that they do not burn. Sprinkle with parsley and serve. *Makes 4 servings.*

FAR-EAST VEGETABLES

1 (10 oz.) box frozen vegetables, thawed. (Choose your favorite veggies)
1 Tbs. safflower oil
⅛ tsp. soy sauce
¼ tsp. peeled, minced garlic

Use nonstick cooking spray on frying pan. Place pan over low heat. Add oil, soy sauce and garlic. Add vegetables and distribute evenly in pan. Cover and cook for approximately 10 minutes, but continue to check and stir periodically. *Serves 4.*

FROTHY, FRUITY DRINKS

You'll need a blender for these thirst quenchers.

BANANA-STRAWBERRY SMOOTHIE*

1 cup milk
¼ cup dry milk
1 banana
1 cup strawberries
2 to 3 ice cubes

Blend all the ingredients together on high speed. *Serves 2.*

PEACH AND RASPBERRY YOGURT SMOOTHIE*

½ cup raspberry yogurt
1 cup milk
1 peach, cut up
4 ice cubes

Blend all the ingredients together on high speed. *Serves 2.*

PEACH MILKSHAKE*

½ cup peach slices, drained
¾ cup vanilla ice cream
1 tsp. orange juice
¼ tsp. vanilla
⅓ cup milk

Blend all ingredients together on high speed. *Serves 1.*

MORE SUPER LOW-SUGAR SWEETS

CARROT CAKE*

3 cups whole-wheat flour, or white flour, or a combination of
    the two
1½ tsp. baking powder
1 tsp. baking soda
1 Tbs. cinnamon
½ tsp. ground cloves
½ tsp. ground ginger
1 (8 oz.) can unsweetened, crushed pineapple, drained
1 (6 oz.) can pineapple juice concentrate, no sugar added
½ cup buttermilk
½ cup honey
2 tsp. vanilla
3 eggs
2½ cups grated carrots
½ cup vegetable oil
1 cup chopped walnuts
1 cup raisins

Sift together dry ingredients into a large bowl and set aside. In
a separate bowl beat eggs; add oil, buttermilk, honey, pineapple juice concentrate and vanilla, mixing well. Add liquid

mixture to dry mixture, again mixing well. Add crushed pine-apple, carrots, and mix. Fold in walnuts and raisins. Pour into an oiled and floured 9″ x 13″ baking pan. Bake at 350 degrees for 55 to 60 minutes. Cool and cut into squares.

BREAD PUDDING*

1 cup dry bread crumbs (make your own by cutting up slices of bread and chopping in a blender)
1½ cups low-fat or skim milk
2 tsp. honey
½ tsp. cinnamon
2 Tbs. raisins
2 eggs, lightly beaten
1 tsp. vanilla

Soak bread crumbs in scalded milk for about 5 minutes. Add honey, cinnamon and raisins. Pour bread mixture over beaten eggs; add vanilla. Pour into oiled baking dish. Bake in 325 degree oven for 50 minutes, or until firm.

PEAR-OATMEAL MUFFINS*

1 (16 oz.) can pear halves (in juice)
1½ cups flour
2 tsp. baking powder
¼ tsp. baking soda
1 tsp. cinnamon
1 cup uncooked oatmeal
½ cup flaked coconut
2 tsp. grated orange peel
1 egg, lightly beaten
⅓ cup honey
¼ cup vegetable oil

Drain pears, setting aside ¼ cup juice. Chop finely. Stir together flour, baking powder, baking soda, cinnamon, oatmeal, coconut and orange peel. Put aside. Blend egg, pear juice (which you set aside), honey and oil. Add to flour mixture and blend well. Stir in pears. Fill greased muffin tins two-thirds full. Sprinkle top with cinnamon (optional). Bake at 400 degrees for 20-25 minutes, or until a wooden toothpick inserted in muffin comes out clean. *Makes 12 muffins.*

Recipes courtesy of Gail Meinhold, R.D.

How Much Food Is Right for You?

*F*or as long as she could remember, fourteen-year-old Kelly had tried her best to follow her parents' advice to eat "three square meals" every day. She knew that, as a growing girl, her maturing body had certain nutritional needs that could be met only by eating nutritious foods from the Four Basic Food Groups.

Kelly tried her best to eat everything she was supposed to every day, but she was rarely able to finish all the good food on her plate. Halfway through the meal, she'd get full and couldn't eat another bite. Her mom would bug her about it and Kelly would bug her mom about bugging her. The worst part was that just about an hour or two later, Kelly would begin to feel hungry again. Of course, when Kelly complained about her hunger symptoms, her mom would only say, "Well, if you would just eat everything that you were supposed to eat. . . ."

Finally, Kelly's best friend, Sharon, came up with a brilliant solution to help end the "hunger-pang problem," as they'd begun to call it.

"Just break up your three big meals into smaller ones," Sharon recommended.

Sharon's suggestion was such a simple one—and yet it was the very thing that Kelly needed. Sharon knew something that even many adults don't know: When it comes to meals, there's no magic in the number three. You can eat as *few* as three larger meals, or as *many* as six smaller meals a day—and still be eating healthily. The key is not to leave out any of the foods you need each day.

So instead of trying to cram all of her food into three sittings, Kelly saved some of her food for snacks and mini-meals throughout the day. Here's one way you can break up big meals into smaller ones, and still get your nourishment:

BREAKFAST 7:30 A.M.
Piece of whole-wheat toast (1 bread)
Cup of low-fat plain yogurt (1 milk)

MID-MORNING SNACK 10:00 A.M.
Apple (1 fruit)
1 Serving of low-fat cheese, such as part-skim
  mozzarella (1 milk)

LUNCH 12:30 P.M.
Tuna sandwich (1 meat, 2 bread)
Vegetable (1 vegetable)
Low-fat or skim milk (1 milk)

AFTER-SCHOOL SNACK 3:30 P.M.
Pear (1 fruit)
1 Serving of crackers (1 bread)
Beverage

DINNER 6:00 P.M.
Small green salad (½ vegetable)
Chicken (1 meat)
Half portion of vegetable (½ vegetable)

AFTER-DINNER STUDYING SNACK 9:00 P.M.
1 Serving dry-roasted nuts (1 meat)

Now it's your turn. The questionnaire below will help you evaluate whether you should stick with three square meals or do as Kelly decided to do—make yours mini-meals. Much of this will depend on how much you can eat, when you get hungry and just how hungry you get. If, for example, you're one of those people who can't sleep on an empty stomach, you might reserve one of your fruit servings for right before bedtime. If you're an athlete, you might want to refuel after your afternoon workout.

Important: If you tend to feel at all dizzy, shaky, headachy, or nauseous between meals, tell your parents and go see your doctor.

☆☆ **HOW MANY MEALS** ☆☆
SHOULD I EAT? QUIZ

1. *I am hungry soon after I finish a regular meal (breakfast, lunch, dinner).*
   Yes   No

2. *I tend to get tired between regular meals.*
   Yes   No

3. *I'm afraid that my "mini-meals" would turn into "major meals"—and that I'd just keep eating.*
   Yes   No

4. *If I go for more than a few hours without food, I feel headachy, weak and shaky.*
   Yes   No

5. *When I'm hungry, I can be a real grouch.*
   Yes   No

6. *I find it...............to finish a regular-sized meal.*
   a.) almost impossible
   b.) all too easy
   c.) not a problem

7. *My daily schedule is so hectic that I barely have time to eat all the nutritious foods I should.*
   Yes   No

☆☆☆

To determine if you need to eat more than three times a day, review your answers to the questions above. If you answered *yes* to three or more of these questions—1,2,4,5,7—and selected "A" for question 6, try to eat at least four times a day. If eating four smaller meals doesn't bring relief, five or six even smaller ones will do the trick.

50

If you answered *no* to three or more of the same questions—1,2,4,5,7, and selected "B" or "C" for question 6, then "three square meals" are probably sufficient for you. *Again, we stress talking to your parents and your doctor before changing your eating patterns.*

YOUR METABOLISM AND WHAT IT MEANS

Why is it that some people can eat all they want— and never put on a pound? Others say that if they even *look* at food, they gain weight. There are lots of reasons for this—as you might guess. But one big reason is *metabolism*.

Metabolism. It's one of those words you've heard a million times, but do you know what it really means? We've talked about how your body is like an engine, or a car. Feed it the right foods, and you'll get lots of mileage out of it. Feed it second-rate fuel, and you'll be runnin' on empty before you know it. Therefore, you might think of your metabolism as the speed at which your motor (your body) runs. Because every human being is a different "model," every one of us has a different metabolic rate. For some people, the motor runs fast. For others, it runs slow.

Even when you think you're doing nothing (like sleeping), your body's hard at work. Your lungs fill with air, your heart pumps blood. It takes energy to perform all of these functions—and that energy is measured in *calories*. Someone who has a fast metabolism is going to burn calories more quickly than someone who has a slow metabolism. Just as you inherited your brown or blue eyes, you inherited your metabolic rate as well. A couple more facts about metabolism:

- Females tend to have a slower metabolism than males.
- You can increase your metabolism by exercising, and slow it down by being sedentary. So don't be a couch potato, get in shape and your body will perform better!
- As you get older, your metabolic rate slows down.

Metabolism is one of the factors that determines how quickly you gain or lose weight—something that seems to concern lots of girls-on-the-grow like you. As adolescent girls begin to develop, they do so at different speeds—something you've undoubtedly noticed, whether you're the "shorty" in your group or the "daddy longlegs." Some of your friends may be plumper than you, and some as skinny as spaghetti. Some probably put on weight faster than others, too. When it comes to this last area, just so you know, metabolism has a lot to do with it. A healthy metabolism allows you to eat the proper amount of food someone your age is supposed to eat, exercise moderately and maintain a healthy weight.

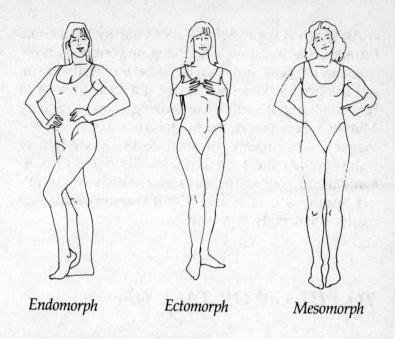

Endomorph   Ectomorph   Mesomorph

BODY TYPES: WHICH ONE ARE YOU?

Just as you're born with your own individual metabolism, you're also born with the predisposition for a certain type of body. Although there are, literally, millions of differently shaped and sized bodies in the world, there are just three basic body types:

- ✪ The *endomorph* has a body that's more curvaceous, and perhaps also broader.
- ✪ The *ectomorph* has a smaller-boned body, and one that generally appears narrower.
- ✪ The *mesomorph* has a build that falls in middle range of the other two in terms of frame size, but is often more muscular.

53

Although it is possible to alter your metabolic rate through exercise, there's no changing your body type. You can eat well and exercise to be the best you can be. The trouble comes when you aim for your body to be something it can't—like striving to be a Skinny Minnie when you're meant to have a few curves. Bigger doesn't mean you have to be overweight or unhealthy. At the same time, smaller doesn't necessarily mean your shape's in shape. That's where eating healthy comes in and why it's so important—no matter what body type you have.

TO PUT ON OR TAKE OFF

Just admit it: Adolescence can be a pretty strange time in your life. "Strange" doesn't necessarily mean "bad" in this case, it just means that you're going through so many changes—both emotional and physical—that it can be a bit overwhelming. You're leaving the world of childhood, although in many ways you are still a child. At the same time, you're beginning the road to womanhood, but you're not quite a woman. So where does that leave you? In between.

Two questions, in particular, wrack the brains of every adolescent girl: The first is, "What's happening to me?" and the second is "Am I normal?" Eventually, you get answers to the first question—with the help of family, teachers, friends and books like this. But the second question is a bit more tricky and it gets asked over and over and over again: about height, about weight, about breast size—and even about hair color.

A changing body, undoubtedly, brings the greatest number of "Am I normal?" questions. One day, when you and your classmates are undressing for gym, you suddenly notice that you're the only girl with developed breasts—or the only one without them. Then your best friend announces that she's gotten her period—and you haven't. Or maybe it's the other way around. The point is, like it or not, this time of your life is comparison time, and the "Am I normals?" that accompany it are, well . . . perfectly normal, too. What prompts the questions, of course, is that girls' bodies don't become more womanlike in unison. Some do a lot of their changing earlier, some do it later. Even if you haven't yet noticed any outward, visible changes, you can bet that they're already starting to occur inside your body.

So, where does nutrition fit in with all this talk about change? As we've said over and over in this book: There's an unshakable connection between a healthy diet and a healthy body. And since, at the moment, your body's doing big things on the growth front, nutrition couldn't be more important. (Did you know this—that the only time you grew *more* quickly is when you were a baby?)

Finally, some girls seem to keep their "little girl shape" a little longer than others. There's nothing wrong with that at all. Remember, this isn't a race. Yet, because many of these same girls are so anxious and eager to "fill out," they eat more of what's *not* good for them, thinking it'll speed the process.

Amanda, a seventh-grader who's somewhat on the

skinny side, said she tried eating five scoops of chocolate ice cream every night before she went to bed, hoping the extra calories would go where she "needed them." She soon learned that this strategy didn't encourage bigger breasts and curves, just extra weight. If you really want to ensure yourself a beautiful body (whether it's petite or statuesque), your best bet is to eat healthy . . . and give yourself some time to grow!

UNDERWEIGHT? OVERWEIGHT? HOW TO TELL

Weight worries. As you've seen, they often accompany puberty. The usual outcry is either, "I'm too fat" or "I'm too skinny." But what exactly is too fat? And what is too skinny?

Remember the three body types: the ectomorph, endomorph and mesomorph? Well, your ideal weight depends upon which type you are. An endomorph who's four foot seven will probably weigh more than an ectomorph who's the same height. That doesn't mean the endomorph is necessarily fat, though. Her bigger bones and larger frame demand more weight. In fact, depending on both girls' eating and exercise habits, the endomorph may even be *leaner*—have a lower *percentage* of body fat—than the thinner-looking ectomorph.

Is there a perfect weight for everyone? Yes, give or take a few pounds. The chart on the opposite page gives an estimate of the ideal weight for numerous height/age combinations. Since you know that people grow at different rates, understand that the figures on this chart should be used as a guide only. Also, they do not account for body type/frame size.

GIRLS' HEIGHT/WEIGHT CHART*

I Am This Tall (feet/inches)	AGE (years) 8	9	10	11	12	13	14	15	16
3-foot-7	40								
3-foot-8	42								
3-foot-9	45								
3-foot-10	47	47	47						
3-foot-11	49	50	50						
4-feet	52	52	52	52					
4-foot-1	54	55	55	56					
4-foot-2	57	58	58	60	60				
4-foot-3	60	60	61	62	62				
4-foot-4	63	63	63	64	66				
4-foot-5	66	67	67	67	68	70			
4-foot-6	68	70	70	71	71	73			
4-foot-7		73	74	74	75	77	78		
4-foot-8		76	78	78	79	80	84		
4-foot-9			81	82	82	84	89	93	
4-foot-10			84	87	86	88	93	96	100
4-foot-11			87	91	90	93	97	101	104
5-feet				95	96	97	101	105	108
5-foot-1				97	101	101	105	108	112
5-foot-2					105	106	108	112	114
5-foot-3					110	111	112	115	116
5-foot-4					114	115	117	118	120
5-foot-5						120	120	121	124
5-foot-6						124	125	126	128
5-foot-7						127	129	131	133
5-foot-8							131	133	134
5-foot-9							133	135	136
5-foot-10							134	136	138

(*Adapted from World Health Organization data)

Your weight may be an emotional issue for you, and you may not be able to look at yours objectively. If you are obviously fat or feel you are overweight, you should go to a doctor. If you weigh too much, the doctor will let you know, and may put you on a supervised diet. You should *NEVER* take it upon yourself to go on any kind of strict diet. This is crucial, as almost all doctors and dieticians agree that your teenage growth period is not the time to limit your caloric intake—unless, of course, you're simply eating too much of the wrong foods.

In addition, if you feel at all awkward or uncomfortable about your weight, whether you think you're over- or underweight, ask your doctor for a professional opinion.

Ideally, the smartest way to control your weight is to eat nutritiously: Stick to your recommended daily servings from the Basic Four, cut out items such as empty, sugary calories and excess fats and exercise regularly. Healthy weight control is as simple as that.

SKIPPING MEALS

Meal skipping is a bad idea—period. When you don't eat regularly, your blood sugar takes a dive causing the "yo-yo" effect. Your body will scramble to cope with such a "fuel shortage" by calling out the reserves of stored protein and fat. This can be hard on your poor, hungry body—and you will feel the strain. You may not be as alert, and you may have trouble concentrating.

It's an especially big deal if you skip breakfast. You haven't eaten anything since the night before and when you wake up, your body's running on empty, and is ready to have its fuel supply restocked. So, is breakfast important? You betcha! Finally, keep in mind that when you do skip a meal, it's this same body—*yours*—that gets shortchanged.

CRASH! BANG! BOOM!
THE CRAZINESS OF CRASH DIETS

Some people skip meals not because they wake up late, not because they're busy, not because they "forget," but because they believe that doing so will help them lose weight. Nothing could be further from the truth. In fact, people who diet by not eating—or not eating enough, as in the case of many so-called "crash diets"—seem to be setting themselves up for weight gain. They may lose weight at first—mostly in the form of water, not fat—but they'll soon put it right back on. Consequently, the lose-gain cycle continues. Why? Because when you eat less, your body learns to get by on less. In response, your metabolism slows down. When this happens you burn calories more slowly and gain weight more easily.

The only way to a permanent weight loss is to eat healthfully—not necessarily less—and exercise more. You'll love the results—and better yet, they'll last.

DISTORTED IMAGES

Everywhere you look, whether it's television or magazines, the topic is losing weight and dieting. America's obsession with dieting has infiltrated just about every nook and cranny of today's society. Most likely, diet discussion takes place in your school, too.

It's no wonder, then, that so many girls worry about their weight. They've heard the "thin is in" message loud and clear. The tragic result is that many young women who are at their ideal weight think they should weigh less.

But is "thin" in? Even a couple of years ago, one glance at a fashion magazine said, "Yes." The skin-and-bones look was the order of the day. But open up the same magazine today, and you're likely to see a somewhat different picture: models who have curves, muscles and sometimes more than a bit of meat on their bones. The new model message is this: Fit is fashionable, and a healthy, well-fed, well-exercised body is best.

So, put on your workout clothes, grab an apple and *forget* about dieting!

OUT-OF-CONTROL WEIGHT CONTROL

As we've discussed, it's normal to wonder—and even worry—about your changing body. But for some girls, worries about weight turn to preoccupation. Why is this?

First of all, adolescence brings with it a number of concerns. You begin to ask questions: Am I popular? Am I smart enough? Am I attractive? Am I a good person? In time, most everybody finds answers to these questions. But for some girls, they cause anger, guilt, sadness—feelings that can seem overpowering. Even worse, these girls can begin to feel as if their emotions are out of their control. Weight is something they can control. Too often, however, the result is an eating disorder.

DESTRUCTIVE DIETING: EATING DISORDERS

In this section, we're going to describe two very serious sicknesses—eating disorders called *anorexia nervosa* and *bulimia*. It's important for you pre-teen and teenage girls to know about these diseases because you are the ones who suffer from them the most.

An anorexic (someone with anorexia) is obsessed with not eating. A girl with this illness will purposely control her food intake—decreasing it to almost nothing—in an attempt to "control" her body. She may also exercise excessively, another method of weight control. The anorexic often starts off simply wanting to lose a few pounds. What happens, though, is that she becomes so preoccupied with the *control* that she loses sight—literally—of what is a proper, *realistic* weight for her. To anyone else's eye, the anorexic appears thin and, often, well below her ideal weight. Yet, when she looks in the mirror, she can only see a "fat person."

Anorexia is self-imposed starvation and it can lead to serious health problems (malnutrition, for one), and in the worst cases—death (an estimated eight percent of those with anorexia die from it). Even when they're aware that they have the disease, though, most anorexics can't stop their destructive behavior—at least not alone. They need professional help. Oddly enough, in their effort to gain control, they lose control.

Bulimia often goes hand in hand with anorexia. A

bulimarectic is someone who suffers from both anorexia and bulimia. Bulimia, known as the binge-purge disease, is called that because bulimics will, literally, gorge on massive quantities of food—sometimes thousands of calories—then rid themselves of it by vomiting and taking laxatives. In a sense, they try to cover up their bad feelings by eating these huge amounts of food. As soon as they finish eating, though, they feel worse—and guilty—and so they purge.

This cycle repeats and repeats. Oddly, the bulimic tends to stay at an almost-normal weight, or may even be somewhat overweight. That's why it can be tough to tell if a person has bulimia. Also, bulimics like to keep their problem hidden from family and friends. Anorexics, on the other hand, usually exhibit telltale signs: most notably, emaciation and an apparent lack of appetite.

Although both illnesses are much more common in girls and women, boys and men can also develop them. Basically, people with eating disorders tend to suffer from low self-esteem—they don't feel very good about themselves. They're hurting inside, but instead of dealing with their emotional selves and their problems, they try to control their physical selves. The outcome can be tragic. Frequent vomiting, especially, can wreak havoc on a body: yellowed and decaying teeth caused by harsh stomach acids, ulcers—even a heart attack, no matter what the age. Anorexia, even without the added trauma of bulimia, can also kill you.

COMPULSIVE OVEREATING

Do you know anyone who eats whenever she does poorly on a test, or when she's had a blow-up with her parents? People like this often use food to soothe or comfort themselves, to "push down" bad feelings. These people may be suffering from a more common eating disorder: compulsive overeating. The danger here is that over a period of time compulsive overeating can lead to obesity, which can cause big-time health problems.

For many compulsive overeaters, food becomes the "answer" to their problems. Instead of confronting a friend they're angry with, or coping with their stress, they eat away their anger. Unfortunately, this doesn't get rid of the anger, which only continues to eat away at them.

Obviously, the eventual goal for a compulsive overeater is to stick to a balanced, nutritious eating plan. Before that's going to happen, though, compulsive overeaters need to face up to what's troubling them.

If you need help in dealing with a particular situation, don't hesitate to ask for it. If you know that you raid the refrigerator after an exam, put yourself somewhere else—not in the kitchen. Here are some fun things you can do to work off stress or extra energy instead of eating:

- ✪ exercise
- ✪ dance
- ✪ sing
- ✪ draw, paint
- ✪ play music

- ✪ wash the car
- ✪ ride a bike
- ✪ walk the dog
- ✪ knit a sweater
- ✪ clean your room

How else can you put a stop to nonstop eating? Be practical. If you know you have a habit of overdoing it with the ice cream in the afternoon, don't say, "I'm not going to have any." You will—and you'll have more than you should. Instead, allow yourself to have a tiny portion.

Troubled feelings often come with pre-teen and teen territory. If they're getting in the way of your healthy eating habits, then you owe it to yourself to make some changes. Think of it this way: *Your health will be better if you're happy, and you'll be happier if you're healthy.*

Food and Fitness

*E*xercise enthusiasts, fitness fanatics . . . call them what you like. They're everywhere—and that's because staying in shape has become big business. Because so many people have been jumping aboard the fitness bandwagon, it's not always easy to get the facts about fitness straight. Before you plunge into the "element of exercise," why not put your fitness knowledge to the test—just to see where you stand? Read the statements below, then decide if they are true or false.

☆☆   FITNESS QUIZ   ☆☆

1. *Thin people don't really need to bother with exercise.*
   True or False

2. *People who exercise on a regular basis generally need to eat more.*
   True or False

3. *After rigorous exercise, your body continues to burn calories for many hours.*
   True or False

4. *Participating in a regular exercise program can give your spirits a lift, and improve your outlook on life.*
   True or False

5. *If you exercise enough, you can eat anything you want—including sugary foods—and not worry about it.*
   True or False

6. *It's not a good idea to exercise during your period.*
   True or False

7. *You should wait an hour or more after you eat before you begin exercising.*
   True or False

8. *Sweating is a good sign that your exercise of choice is "working."*
   True or False

9. *Exercise has to hurt to be helpful (the "no pain, no gain" theory).*
   True or False

10. *Only aerobic exercise is worth doing.*
    True or False

Answers: 1. False 2. True 3. True 4. True 5. False
6. False 7. True 8. False 9. False 10. False

☆☆☆

THE ELEMENT OF EXERCISE: WHY EATING WELL ISN'T ENOUGH

Healthful eating is only part of what contributes to making you feel fit as a fiddle. All the good food in the world—by itself—isn't enough to keep your heart strong and your muscles tight. In fact, if you just kept eating and eating, and didn't do any kind of exercise, eventually all those calories would catch up with you.

That's why you need the winning combination in your life, the "Terrific Twosome": eating healthy and *exercising*. The two really do go hand in hand. Not only will a regular exercise program make you feel better now, but you will reap the benefits of fitness in your future.

EXERCISE: WHAT IT DOES FOR YOU

How does exercise figure into your own life? Do you exercise daily, or just on weekends, or only every once in a while—like when the gang gets together for a volleyball game? Recent studies have shown that young people—pre-teens and teens—are more out of shape than ever before. If exercise isn't a part of your regular routine now, it's time you learned why it should be.

MAKE A MUSCLE

You were born with muscles, but unless you work those muscles, they'll be squishy and soft. Stomach muscles, for instance, play a big part in supporting your back and keeping your posture straight. But because many people don't bother to strengthen their stomach muscles with exercise, they tend to get soft. As a result, they can't do their job as well. You may know a person who has a potbelly—one not-too-attractive consequence of too much food and not enough exercise.

In the same way that not moving a muscle will soften it, toning or strengthening a muscle with exercise builds lean muscle tissue, which feels and looks firmer. Having healthy muscles—not necessarily big ones—is simply part of having a healthy body.

HAVE A HEART

Your heart is perhaps the most important muscle in your entire body. It tick-tick-ticks away tirelessly, pumping blood to every part of your body, carrying life-sustaining oxygen along with it. The heart, like any other muscle, needs exercise—in this case, to make it pump more efficiently. *Aerobic* exercise is any kind of exercise that significantly increases the rate at which your heart pumps. Aerobic exercise, such as running, swimming and jumping rope, uses your major muscle groups, i.e. in your arms and legs. To benefit from the effects of aerobic exercise, you need to:

✪ Do it at least three times a week.
✪ "Keep it going" (don't stop the "aerobicizing") for twenty to thirty minutes.

Your heart will be stronger and healthier!

LOVE THOSE LUNGS

Aerobic exercise will also help improve your lung capacity for oxygen. Ever run a race and found you could barely catch your breath? All is not lost. Although being in tip-top shape takes time and dedication, the good news is that you don't have to be a super-jock to be in shape. Find a way to fit *your* form of fitness to your lifestyle.

GET PLENTY OF AEROBIC EXERCISE AND YOU'LL ALSO:

✪ Maintain your weight.
✪ Sleep better.
✪ Be more resistant to illness.
✪ Lower your chances for heart disease.
✪ Improve your circulation.
✪ Keep depression at bay.
✪ Increase your energy level.
✪ Boost your ability to concentrate.
✪ Release tension and stress.
✪ Look more radiant.
✪ Feel more alert and alive.

What do you think? All this good health and a beautiful body, too? Sounds like a pretty generous payoff—and it's yours for the asking. So why not get moving?

DOCTOR'S ORDERS

We strongly recommend that everyone who wants to start an exercise program should consult a doctor first. This is vital for people who are overweight, have medical problems, or haven't been exercising regularly. Your pediatrician, family doctor or school physician can do the honors. He or she may also be able to give you advice about good exercise choices for you. Once you've been given a clean bill of health, you can be on your way to feeling fit—and fabulous. If fitness already is a way of life for you, hurray!

"BURN" CALORIES AND BUILD A STRONGER BODY

If you're ready to experience the excitement of exercise, here are a few pointers to get you off on the right foot:

CHOOSE A FORM OF EXERCISE THAT YOU'LL ENJOY

If you hate running, but decide to start doing it because it's "good for you," then you're setting yourself up for failure. You probably won't last more than a few workouts. Check out the activity chart that follows. Surely there's something on it that will sound like fun to you. If your first choice flops, don't give up: Try something else. Sorry, shopping doesn't count as vigorous exercise.

DON'T GO OVERBOARD AT FIRST

If you really want to make exercise part of your permanent health plan, don't blow it by overdoing it—unless you want unnecessarily sore muscles or worse, injuries. Also, don't expect too much, too soon. Give yourself a chance to build up stamina and strength. Start out slowly and gradually increase your activity level. Remember, exercise doesn't have to hurt to be helpful.

Stretching is the key to healthy exercise.

STRETCH FOR SUCCESS

It's not wise to begin any exercise "cold"—that is, without warming up. Begin your warm-up waking your body up slowly. Start walking slowly and, after a couple of minutes, walk at a faster pace. Do this for five minutes and then you can begin your stretching exercises. Stretching when your muscles aren't "warm" can cause injury. To prevent tight muscles, you'll also want to stretch at the end of your exercise session.

To give you an idea of how many calories a certain activity burns (per hour), see the chart on the next page. Keep in mind that the figures are estimates and will vary depending on your age and weight. The younger or heavier you are, the more calories you consume in any given activity. Girls also tend to burn off fewer calories than boys, so the lower end of the scale will probably be more accurate for you.

Warm up first, your body will thank you!

ACTIVITY LEVEL	CALORIES USED PER HOUR	ACTIVITIES
Sedentary	80 to 110	Reading Writing Watching TV Eating
	110 to 150	Walking, slowly Cooking Painting
Light	150 to 240	Ironing Dancing, slowly
Moderate	240 to 300	Walking, moderate Gardening, light Bowling Fishing Food shopping Cycling, slowly Mopping floors
	300 to 360	Walking, faster than normal Table tennis (ping-pong) Cycling Tennis, doubles Badminton Calisthenics
Vigorous	360 to 420	Walking, briskly Cycling, fast Ice skating Roller skating Tennis, singles
	420 to 480	Waterskiing Horseback riding, trotting Dancing, folk or popular
	480 to 600	Jogging, slowly Horseback riding, galloping Speed cycling Downhill skiing Basketball
Strenuous	600 to 660	Running, 5.5 mph Swimming, breaststroke
	More than 660	Running, more than 6 mph Squash Handball Cross-country skiing

Source: Ventura County (Calif.) Health Care Agency

FIT OR FLABBY:
THE CHOICE IS YOURS

Twelve-year-old Lisa admits that although she gets plenty of exercise, she's still a little bit overweight. "I'm not fat," says Lisa, "just plump. I thought that if I exercised enough, I could eat whatever I wanted."

Lisa had found a way to incorporate exercise into her life (walking and bicycling), but she hadn't learned to cut back on the amount of sugar-filled and fatty foods she ate. As a result, she was stuck with pudge that just wouldn't budge.

If you consume more calories than your body can use in day-to-day functioning and exercise, the extra calories will be stored as fat. For example, a banana split may have as many as 1,250 calories. That doesn't mean you shouldn't ever indulge, but once more, only regular exercise *and* good eating habits add up to a beautiful, healthy body. Leave either one out of the equation and you'll be stuck with more of something you don't want. Forget fitness? You'll end up with a smaller, but flabbier self. Nix nutritious foods in favor of sweet-but-empty calories? You'll see a figure that may be fuller than you'd like.

Shaping up is great; you've seen all the amazing things it can do for you. But don't think of exercise as a replacement for healthful eating. Keep the "Terrific Twosome"—exercise and good eating—together, and you're sure to see the super shape you want!

An Apple a Day…

No doubt about it, your body needs "fuel food" to keep it in the pink. That's right. Many young people like you are learning that a healthy diet is essential for good health. Unfortunately, too many adolescents think that they can eat whatever they want when they're young. They're under the impression that only when they get older will they have to worry about and watch what they eat. Nothing could be further from the truth.

Let's talk again about body fuel and the car engine: Like a car, your body can run on low-grade fuel (less-than-healthful food) as long as it gets enough of it. But you will have to put up with a few minor "knocks" and "pings" along the road. Over the long haul (several years), a car—or a body—that hasn't been taken care of isn't going to win any races, if you know what I mean. So, doesn't it make sense to give your body high-grade fuel so that your body will be a winner? You bet it does!

THE KEY TO A HEALTHY HEART

What you eat *now* definitely matters, and it especially matters as far as the future health of your heart. In fact, evidence shows that a person's eating habits during the later teen years and early twenties may often set the stage for a disease called *atherosclerosis*, which is coronary heart disease. What exactly is this? Well, you know what arteries are. They're the pipe-like vessels inside you that supply oxygen-rich blood to your body's tissues and organs. The process of atherosclerosis begins when excess fat from your diet gets deposited in your artery walls. These deposits are also linked to cholesterol—not a fat, but a substance associated with animal products like eggs and meat. A normal, or "clean" fat-free artery will allow blood to flow through freely. But when an artery or vessel gets too blocked up with fat, it becomes smaller and narrows, and blood can't pass through as easily.

Finally, if too much fat builds up in a particular area, the artery can become hardened and less elastic, and, eventually, completely clogged—so that very little or no blood can get to the place it needs to go. This becomes a cause of great concern when the arteries going to the heart become blocked. Ultimately, this can even cause a heart attack.

Believe it or not, nutrition experts have labeled today's teens the "next generation of heart attack victims" because of the excessive amount of fat-laden and sugary foods many of them consume. Other factors that may put a person at risk for coronary heart disease (CHD) include:

- ✪ genetic predisposition (Has anyone in your family died from CHD?)
- ✪ smoking
- ✪ obesity (being extremely overweight)
- ✪ not enough regular exercise
- ✪ stress
- ✪ high level of cholesterol
- ✪ high blood pressure (see below for more)

Fortunately, you're learning about nutrition now, *before* you're an adult. Although you can't change your genetic makeup, it is possible to make other changes—healthy changes—in your life. If you can begin to practice habits for a healthy heart *now* (good nutrition and exercise), you may be able to prevent atherosclerosis—and let those awesome arteries continue to do an excellent job.

OBESITY

What distinguishes an obese person from someone who is just overweight? Obesity is defined as the condition of being extremely overweight—usually twenty percent or more over your normal, healthy weight. Being overweight, even if you're not obese, can cause several health problems: heart disease, circulatory troubles, high blood pressure and arthritis. With obesity, not only does the likelihood of these problems increase, but they may be much more severe.

It's estimated that more than forty percent of all children and teens are over their ideal weight. Why? Why do you think? Because they eat too much—too much that's high-fat, high-sugar or high-calorie—and exercise too little. Also, although obesity is generally regarded as a physical problem, it may in part be tied to emotional problems, as in the case of compulsive overeating. And certainly, being extremely overweight can take its toll on a person's emotional well-being.

Your body stores any excess calories as fat. The truth, however, is that many overweight young people do not eat more than their normal-weight friends. Many overweight girls, in fact, generally consume even *fewer* calories than their leaner friends. That leaves only one possibility: that the overweight kids tend to be less physically active.

The solution, therefore, lies not in *less* food, but *more* exercise. At a time when your body's making major growth moves, it's vital to consume all the nutrients you need. For this reason, nutrition experts say that for girls in your age group, the best weight-loss technique isn't eating a low-calorie diet, but getting a higher dose of aerobic exercise. If more than thirty percent of your daily calories come from fat, then cutting back on your fat intake to trim excess pounds is acceptable. Don't forget that you do need a tiny amount of fat in your diet.

FIGHTING BACK WITH FIBER

One of the newest buzz words on the nutrition scene is fiber. Basically, fiber is a complex carbohydrate that comes from plant cells. You may be more familiar with the term roughage—it's the same thing. Fiber-rich foods include whole-grain breads and cereals, fresh fruits and vegetables, nuts and dried beans.

So what's all the fuss about fiber, and what's its connection to good health? Unlike most of the other foods that pass through your digestive system, fiber is not broken down (digested). And your body benefits from this? You bet! Fiber provides "bulk," which aids in waste passage. So a high-fiber diet speeds up the whole waste-passage process. This is what has led doctors to believe that a diet that's high in fiber will lower your chances of certain kinds of colorectal cancers—cancers of the colon and rectum.

Conversely, a *high-fat diet* has been indicated as a contributing factor to colon cancers, as well as other forms of the disease. Because these cancers develop inside the digestive tract—and fiber is good at cleansing the bowels—more fiber means less time for cancer-conducive agents to stay in your body.

Another reason for the fiber frenzy? According to some doctors, it lowers blood cholesterol levels by sort of interfering with, or getting in the way of, cholesterol being absorbed. Although there's less proof on this point, there's no doubt that fiber makes for fabulous food. So, make sure you get your daily fill:

twenty-five to forty grams a day. The following chart will give you an idea of how much fiber certain foods provide:

Foods and the amount of dietary fiber they contain*

Food	Amount	Grams of Dietary Fiber
Fruits		
Apple (w/skin)	1 medium	3.5
Banana	1 medium	2.4
Cantaloupe	¼ melon	1.0
Cherries, sweet	10	1.2
Peach (w/skin)	1	1.9
Pear (w/skin)	½ large	3.1
Prunes	3	3.0
Raisins	¼ cup	3.1
Raspberries	½ cup	3.1
Strawberries	1 cup	3.0
Orange	1 medium	2.6
Vegetables, cooked		
Asparagus, cut	½ cup	1.0
Broccoli	½ cup	2.2
Brussels sprouts	½ cup	2.3
Parsnips	½ cup	2.7
Potato (w/skin)	1 medium	2.5
Spinach	½ cup	2.1
String beans, green	½ cup	1.6
Sweet potato	½ medium	1.7
Turnip	½ cup	1.6
Zucchini	½ cup	1.8
Vegetables, raw		
Celery, diced	½ cup	1.1
Cucumber	½ cup	0.4
Lettuce, chopped	1 cup	0.9
Mushrooms, sliced	½ cup	0.9
Tomato	1 medium	1.5
Spinach	1 cup	1.2

Food	Amount	Grams of Dietary Fiber
Legumes, cooked		
Baked beans	½ cup	8.8
Dried peas	½ cup	4.7
Kidney beans	½ cup	7.3
Lima beans	½ cup	4.5
Lentils	½ cup	3.7
Navy beans	½ cup	6.0
Breads, pastas and flours		
Bagels	1 bagel	0.6
Bran muffins	1 muffin	2.5
French bread	1 slice	0.7
Oatmeal bread	1 slice	0.5
Pumpernickel bread	1 slice	1.0
Whole wheat bread	1 slice	1.4
Rice, brown, cooked	½ cup	1.0
Spaghetti, cooked	½ cup	1.1
Nuts and seeds		
Almonds	10 nuts	1.1
Peanuts	10 nuts	1.4
Filberts	10 nuts	0.8
Popcorn, popped	1 cup	1.0
Breakfast cereals		
All-bran type	⅓ cup	8.5
40% bran-type	¾ cup	4.0
Raisin bran-type	¾ cup	4.0
Shredded wheat	⅔ cup	2.6
Oatmeal, cooked	¾ cup	1.6
Cornflakes	1¼ cup	0.3
Meat/Poultry/Fish		0

*Adapted from a critical review of food fiber analysis and data by E. Lanza and R.R. Butron.
Journal of The American Dietetic Association 86:732, 1986.

A BIT ABOUT HIGH BLOOD PRESSURE

Almost any time you go to the doctor for a checkup, one of the first things you do is have your blood pressure checked. Do you know what blood pressure is? Quite simply, it's the "push" created by your heart that circulates blood through your body. What, then, is *high* blood pressure? It's a sign that your heart is having to work extra hard to do its job—to pump your blood. For your heart's health, that's anything but good.

Fortunately, not everyone has high blood pressure, although it is possible to develop it. If you do, your heart won't be happy that your diet contains a lot of *salt* or *sodium*, which can make blood pressure soar even higher. Health problems that are proven to be associated with high blood pressure include heart attacks, kidney disease and strokes.

So it's a good idea to limit your sodium intake. Try to train your taste buds to live without added table salt—after a while, you won't even miss it—and always check food labels for sodium content. A single teaspoon of salt contains 2,300 milligrams of sodium. Consider, though, that on a daily basis, you need just 1,000 milligrams of sodium for every 1,000 calories you eat. Not much room left for lots of salt shaking. Canned soups tend to be heavily laden with sodium, but you'll also be surprised to find it in such foods as breakfast cereals, certain cheeses, microwavable meals and salad dressings.

Sodium also makes your body retain fluids. Yes, this can make you feel bloated, but fluid retention can lead to much more serious health problems. One more reason to shake the salt habit.

THE CALCIUM CONNECTION

You've already heard about the so-called "calcium

connection." But did you know that insufficient doses of calcium can contribute to osteoporosis, a disease that causes thinning of the bones throughout the body? Calcium deficiency is also associated with what's known as "dowager's hump" (a rounded bump on the upper back that interferes with normal, upright posture), a condition that may afflict older people, particularly women.

Because osteoporosis affects one out of every four women over the age of sixty-five, you'll be doing yourself a big favor by "boning up" on your knowledge of calcium-rich foods. Pre-teen and teen girls should aim to include approximately 1,000 milligrams of calcium in their daily diet. Prevention of osteoporosis begins early on in childhood, and during your teen years it becomes even more important to eat calcium-rich foods.

THE CALCIUM CONNECTION

How Much Calcium (in milligrams)?

1 cup of ricotta cheese (part skim)	669 mg.
1 cup of nonfat yogurt	452 mg.
3 oz. salmon (fresh, cooked)	355 mg.
1 cup of almonds	304 mg.
1 cup of low-fat milk	300 mg.
1 cup of chocolate pudding	265 mg.
1 stalk of broccoli, cooked	158 mg.
1 cup of peanuts	107 mg.

NUTRITION IN A NUTSHELL

YOUR HEALTH: WHAT YOU CAN DO
TO MAKE A DIFFERENCE

The United States Department of Agriculture, together with the United States Department of Health and Human Services, has put together a list of "Dietary Guidelines for Americans." As you'll see when you read them, they provide a good overview of much of what you've learned so far about eating healthy.

DIETARY GUIDELINES FOR AMERICANS

- ❂ Eat a variety of foods.
- ❂ Maintain a desirable weight.
- ❂ Avoid too much fat, saturated fat and cholesterol.
- ❂ Eat foods with adequate starch and fiber.
- ❂ Avoid too much sugar.
- ❂ Avoid too much sodium.

You might call these "rules to live by" because they sum up the basics of good nutrition. Although some factors for good health, such as heredity, are out of your control, it's nice to know that you can have quite a lot of input when it comes to the business of your body. The choice is yours, so why not be good to it?

Good Food and Looking Good

BEAUTY: MORE THAN SKIN DEEP

*I*t's true: The right hairstyle, makeup and clothes can do wonders for your appearance, but if you really want to improve your pretty potential—permanently—you can't possibly pass up nutrition.

When people say that "beauty is more than skin deep," they're not kidding. True beauty does radiate from within—and eating nutritiously is where it all begins. It's true that you can't ignore the "appearance impact" of personality: A happy, upbeat, pleasant personality can help a plain-looking girl look pretty, and a pretty girl look *gorgeous*. It's this inner beauty of your spirit and soul which will also come shining through to your surface. But healthy eating makes for good health—and a happy, healthy you!

You're at the age when finding the right look really matters. You want to look good—for yourself, and maybe even (dare we say it) for the boys! And yet, so many growing girls sabotage their looks because they don't get enough of the good food they need. Back to our car example for a minute: You can frequent the car wash, polish the fenders—even give the chassis a new paint job—but if you don't keep up with engine maintenance, the car isn't going to serve you very well when you need it. It's the same with your body—and your looks. Even if you are lucky enough to be able to hire a makeup artist, a hairstylist and a fashion consultant to give you a whole new, beautiful look, it's likely that you won't look your absolute *best* if you aren't feeding your body with genuine "beauty fuel"—in the form of *healthful foods*.

NUTRITION: THE BEAUTY BASIC

SKIN STUFF

Do you have any idea what the largest organ in your body is? Lungs? Intestines? Nope. It's your *skin*. Strangely enough, at about the same time that you

86

start to care more about how you look, your skin may start breaking out. Why is this? In part, because of chemicals in your body known as *hormones*. Hormones help bring on puberty, and in doing so, they also prime the oil glands in your skin to start pumping more sticky stuff called *sebum*. When excess sebum and dirt combine, the result is sometimes those pesty little things called pimples. But other factors, such as heredity, stress, cleansing habits, sleep and oil-based cosmetics, can also affect the appearance of your skin.

What else do you think affects the condition of your skin? Nutrition, of course.

A dermatologist (skin doctor) will tell you that there is no absolute proof that eating certain foods—such as sweets, chips, or fried foods—will cause skin breakouts, or acne. But if you find that your breakouts seem to coincide with your having eaten specific foods, the doctor may advise you to cut back on them.

While eating a balanced, healthy diet can't cure acne, it can improve the appearance of your skin in other ways: softer texture, rosier cheeks, and a "healthy glow." Foods that are rich in Vitamin A and the B-complex vitamins are said to be essential for your skin's health. And if you've ever seen a fashion model's list of beauty secrets, it almost always includes the "skin saver"—drinking plenty of water.

The connection between a poor diet and skin problems is not the result of the food that *is* going into your body but, rather, the food that *isn't*. Remember, if you're eating too many empty calories, you're probably not getting enough of the nutritious calories you need. Think of that next time you glance in the mirror.

A TIP FOR TIP-TOP TRESSES AND
NEWS FOR KNOCK-OUT NAILS

The girl with the perfect hair. How many times have you watched her walking down the school halls—hair blowing, bouncing, shining—and said something to the effect of, *Oh, what I wouldn't do for a head of hair like that!*? To a large degree, you have good ol' Mom and Dad's genes to thank—or blame—for your hair (color, texture, etc.). While you can't change that part of the deal, you can give your hair something to grow on: good food. Actually, everyone's hair grows at a different rate, but healthy hair generally tends to grow faster than unhealthy hair.

Your hair, as well as your fingernails and toenails, is ninety-eight percent protein. Not surprisingly, eating a balanced diet that includes protein turns out to be one of the best beauty treatments for a strong, shiny mane, and strong nails. Dull, lank hair may also indicate a lack of vitamin B_{12}. So, you can lather all you like with luxurious shampoos and conditioners, but remember: As far as your hair's concerned, what you put *inside* your body will make a bigger difference than anything you put on your head.

TERRIFIC TEETH

Without your teeth, eating healthy (eating—period!) would be a tough task. But your teeth aren't the only things in your mouth that need taking care of: You've also got those pink gums to think about. If your gums go, then you know what's gonna go next.

One substance in your diet especially affects your dental health: sugar. And if you've ever had a cavity filled, you know that it's not something to look forward to. Cavities may cause discomfort, but what's the greater cause for concern? Here, gum disease takes the cake. How to prevent it? It's okay to have sweet treats occasionally, but when you do, you should brush your teeth afterwards. In addition, flossing, regular (biannual) checkups and a good, healthy diet all work together to prevent tooth and gum problems.

Halitosis, or bad breath, is frequently caused by tooth decay and gum problems. Finally, calcium-rich foods will help keep your teeth strong. So what do you say? How about showing them that you're serious about your smile?

FOR GIRLS ONLY

You may or may not have started menstruating—or having your period, as it's commonly referred to. If you haven't yet begun, it's likely that you'll experience your menarche—first menstrual cycle—sometime between the ages of nine and sixteen. If you are already menstruating, then you may know the things that can come along with it: bloating, cramps, headaches and irritability. Though some people experience these problems more than others, paying attention to the food you're eating can help keep such discomforts to a minimum.

First, try to avoid eating salty foods, which make you retain even more water. This is especially important before your period, but you'll be better off if you can make a low-sodium diet a way of life. Whatever salt you do eat will be washed away more quickly if you drink plenty of water.

Also, because you lose blood—and with it, iron—at this time, try to include iron-packed foods in your meals: lean beef; fish; green, leafy vegetables. An iron deficiency can bring on a certain type of *anemia*, a blood condition that decreases the amount of red (oxygen-carrying) blood cells you produce. Anemia may make you feel tired and listless—and who needs that? Once again, eating healthy seems to be just what the doctor ordered.

GET A GLOW FROM THE GREEN

Ever notice how one of the last things to go on most kids' plates (maybe yours, too) are the vegetables? If only you realized what "pretty power" you were passing up. Your body needs every one of the Basic Four Food Groups, but if there's one food you should try to get more of, it's veggies. Few calories, high fiber—and more good news—they give you an all-over glow (and no, not a green one!). So, if you've been looking for an unbeatable beauty secret, look no further.

☆☆　EATING PRETTY QUIZ　☆☆

See how much you've learned about good food and looking good:
1. *Fried, sugary and salty foods are usually to blame for skin breakouts.*
   True or False

2. *Hair and nails are made primarily of protein.*
   True or False
3. *Carrots can improve your vision.*
   True or False
4. *A good shampoo and conditioner are the best beauty treatments for your hair.*
   True or False
5. *Heredity has little to do with what kind of hair—and hair problems—you may have.*
   True or False
6. *Brushing your teeth is sufficient precaution against tooth decay and gum disease.*
   True or False
7. *Foods that have a high sodium content can cause water retention.*
   True or False

Answers: 1. False 2. True 3. False 4. False 5. False 6. False 7. True

"Just Eat It"

*I*magine the following scenario: You're sitting in class at school. It's almost *that time*, and even though your teacher's bound to call on you at any minute, you keep one eye on the clock—thinking that, somehow, doing so will make the time pass more quickly. Finally, the long-awaited signal comes . . . RRRIIIIINNGGG! You scoop up your books, bolt out the door with the rest of your classmates and make a beeline for the cafeteria. Ahhhh, lunch at last!

Do you look forward to lunch, or dinner, or any eating occasion? Do you know why? Your state of hunger is a factor, of course. But hungry or not, meals are also a time for friends, for family, for conversation. That's part of what makes food fun. In short, eating is a social activity.

We discussed earlier how certain relationships, particularly those with your family, can influence what and how you eat. For example, maybe your mom cooks special meals or bakes goodies. Perhaps your friends like to frequent the ice cream shop after school—and, naturally, you're right there along with them when the scoops are ordered. The point is, you probably find yourself in any number of eating situations that don't exactly lend themselves to eating pretty.

HOW TO SAY "NO" WHEN EVERYONE ELSE IS SAYING "YES"

PRESSURE FROM PARENTS AND PEERS

Even as more and more people are beginning to care about the food they put into their tummies, many teens report that food pressures from parents and peers can be a huge stumbling block to healthy eating. Such pressures become particularly problematic if you're a young person who's trying to maintain a healthy weight. Just take a look at the letter below:

Dear Smart Talk,

I've been reading a lot about nutrition lately and want to try to start eating better (I'm a little over-weight). I've asked my mom not to keep so many sweets and other fattening foods around the house, but she still buys them. Both of my parents are always bugging me to eat more and "finish what's on my plate." I sure wish that they'd take me seriously about this.

Can you help?

Sarah

How can you get your family to take your newfound interest in nutrition seriously? You can start by letting them know about it. Sarah had attempted this by asking her mom to purchase fewer sweet snacks and other fattening things, but she never really let her mom in on *why*. Instead, Sarah might have first expressed her concern about her weight, and her desire to eat more healthfully. Then, Sarah could even offer to help her mom with the grocery shopping—and select more nutritious snacks, such as fruit, for herself. Her mom would probably also love to have help in the kitchen. Once Sarah's parents understood that this wasn't just a passing fancy—and that their daughter truly wanted their support in achieving her good-food goals—they would certainly be more likely to do whatever they could to help.

Many people use food as one way of expressing love. Your grandmother, for instance, may think she's doing something nice for you by baking a batch of super-yummy chocolate chip cookies. If chocolate chip cookies aren't a part of your eating plan, you should let her know. Don't wait till she presents you with two dozen to give her the news. A better idea is to say something like, "Grandma, you're such a great cook—and I really love those chocolate chip cookies of yours. But since I'm doing my best to cut back on sugar, maybe you've got another recipe that's just as good, but a little lower in sugar."

This way, you can give your grandmother a compliment, let her know you appreciate her efforts and, at the same time, fill her in on your nutrition news. Both of you benefit. Of course, you can rewrite the "script" to fit your own special food situation.

OF PALS AND PIZZA PARTIES

Like many young people, you've probably gotten the message about saying "NO" to drugs and alcohol. Without a doubt, that's sound advice. Although saying "NO" to something like donuts hardly seems comparable, many girls let their peers push them into eating too much stuff that's not good for them.

Ultimately, of course, it is *you* who decides what foods will go into your mouth. People can invite and push and pressure until they're blue in the face, but if you're committed to a healthy diet, no one can make you eat something you don't want to. The simplest way to avoid this problem is to let your friends know that if and when you say, "No thanks—I don't want any," you really mean it.

Even if your friends don't eat healthy foods—and you're trying to—there's no reason you have to miss out on the fun. When you find yourself confronted with a friend/food dilemma, there are ways to deal with it:

- ✪ You don't have to split an order of french fries with your friend if *you'd* rather have a baked potato.
- ✪ If you're all ordering pizza, you can ask that one half include veggies instead of salty, fatty sausage and pepperoni.
- ✪ When planning get-togethers, why not suggest an "activity outing" instead of one that focuses on food?

Once you've incorporated good nutrition habits into your life, and discovered how much better you can feel, you may be anxious for your family and friends to take up the "good food cause," too. However, nagging people about the "junk" they eat will only backfire and make them eat more of it. If you really want to convince someone else to eat better, your best persuasive tactic is to be a good role model—and eat those good foods yourself.

RESTAURANTS: RULES YOU CAN LIVE WITH

Getting a healthy meal when you eat out isn't hard to do. It simply requires that you: 1. Know how to decipher certain terms on a menu; and 2. Aren't afraid to speak up and ask questions in order to get what you want. Fortunately, as a greater number of Americans develop their "nutrition awareness," more and more restaurants, even fast-food places, are adapting their menus to include healthier choices—and that makes your task easier.

Let's start with the beginning of the meal—which usually starts with bread. Bread is okay to eat—best if it's whole wheat, rye or pumpernickel. The problem comes when you glop on butter, pat after pat. If you can just use a smidgen or, better yet, none at all, you'll be better off. Too tempted? Simple. Just ask your server to take the butter from your table.

OKAY, NOW IT'S TIME TO ORDER:

Waiter/Waitress:	*"What can I get you to drink?"*
✪ Good choices:	Low-fat or skim milk, water, seltzer or fruit juice.
Bad choice:	Soda.

Waiter/Waitress: *"Will you be having soup or salad with your meal?"*

✪ Salad with dressing on the side is probably the wiser choice. Many soups contain lots of salt and fat. So choose carefully—although you can eat just about anything, as long as you do it in moderation.

Waiter/Waitress: *"And for an entrée (main course)?"*

✪ Let's say you love chicken, and since you know it's a good (low-fat) source of protein, you decide to order it. But chicken, like fish, can be prepared in a number of different ways—broiled, grilled and baked are healthy preparations, but fried is not. And a heavy sauce, such as a cream sauce, on the chicken can mean more grams of fat than you might want. If the menu doesn't specify how the food is prepared, *ask* your waiter or waitress.

The American Heart Association suggests you look for these other terms, which indicate that a food has been prepared in a low-fat way:

- ✪ steamed
- ✪ in its own juice
- ✪ garden fresh
- ✪ roasted
- ✪ poached
- ✪ broiled—with lemon juice

Look out for these words which are signs of saturated fat:

- ✪ butter sauce
- ✪ cheese sauce
- ✪ au gratin

- sautéed (similar to fried)
- creamed

Also, if you can, try to go without condiments such as mayonnaise, sour cream, gravy, "special sauce" and other rich additions.

Sharing dessert is a romantic way to cut down on calories.

Waiter/Waitress: *"Will you be having dessert?"*
- Don't worry—you won't have to do without. Fresh fruit is always tasty, and your most nutritious dessert option. Some people just can't seem to stay away from the really sweet stuff, though. If you're

one of them, just share a dessert. That's one way to have your cake and eat it too!

MENU MANIPULATING

If you don't see what you want on the menu, speak up. There's no reason to feel awkward about doing this. You're the customer, after all. For example, if you see only "fried fish" listed, ask your waiter or waitress if you can have it broiled or grilled instead. Even if the only kind of chicken on the menu comes with a white cream sauce, ask if they'll prepare it differently—maybe broiled with lemon juice. Poultry that's cooked without the skin is also lower in fat. If the menu includes a "no-substitutions-please" warning, simply explain that you're on a "special diet." Most places will usually bend the rules.

FAST-FOOD FRENZY: A BEHIND-THE-SCENES LOOK AT THE BURGER BIZ

One place you can't usually custom-order your food? Most of your favorite fast-food joints. Unfortunately, though, if there's one group of foods young people eat too much of, it's this one.

What's wrong with fast food? First, many fast-food meals may be forty to sixty percent fat. If that isn't bad enough, they're also loaded with salt. That's what they *have*.

Now, for what they *don't have*: Fast foods may be seriously lacking in vitamins A and C, as well as fiber.

Do you know what's lurking behind this seemingly innocent meal?

Here's the kind of nutrition you get from a typical fast-food meal:

Food	Calories	Protein (gm)	Fat (gm)	Sodium (mg)
Cheeseburger (large size)	630	32	35	1665
French fries (regular)	220	3	11	109
Milkshake	350	9	8	201
TOTALS	1200	44	54	1975

Surprised? Remember, only *thirty percent* of your daily caloric intake should come from fat. Let's say you eat 2,000 calories a day. That means you should eat sixty-six grams of fat a day. You've already consumed almost your entire day's allotment of fat in this one meal, as well as more than half of your calories!

Don't be too discouraged. You don't have to bag burgers forever. Fast-food dining can be okay, provided that the rest of your meals are nutritionally balanced, and you eat the stuff only two times a week or less. Here's how to make this speedy service work *for* your health, not against it:

- ✪ If a salad bar is a choice, choose it!
- ✪ Choose charbroiled burgers over fried; they have less fat.
- ✪ Build a taco instead of a burger and add lots of veggies.

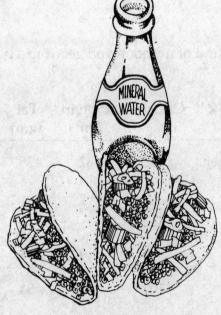

- Stick with the smaller burgers—and hold the mayo, sauce and cheese (which adds an extra 100 calories per slice). Ask for tomato, if available.
- Go for a whole-grain bun, if it's available.
- Forget the fries; pick a baked potato. Go without or go easy on the butter, sour cream and cheese.
- Drink low-fat or nonfat milk, water or seltzer with your meal rather than a milkshake or soda.
- Try frozen yogurt instead of ice cream.

THE SELECT-A-SALAD GUIDE

Even though salad bars are a good choice over burgers and fries, they too can be hiding lots of the things healthy eaters *should* avoid. Here's some help for navigating a safe course at the salad bar:

a. For more nutrients, choose darker green lettuce and fresh spinach over iceberg lettuce.
b. Pile on the veggies—fiber and vitamins galore: broccoli, celery, cauliflower, tomatoes, zucchini, spinach, beets and carrots.
c. Beans, such as kidney and garbanzo, will add a bit of protein POW!
d. Bacon bits, high in sodium and fat, are better left at the salad bar.
e. Rich 'n' creamy salad dressing can kick up the calorie and fat count of your "low-cal" meal. For fewer of both, let "lite" or low-oil dressings dress up your salad.

There you have it: Proof that with a little bit of care—and most of all, moderation—you can still enjoy the convenience and fun of fast food—and *eat pretty, too*.

The Sweet Stuff: Sugar

HOW SWEET IT IS

Had your share of sugar lately? Probably so. The average person eats 134.4 pounds per year! This works out to about two-and-a-half pounds a week, or one-third of a pound (600 calories) a day. Yikes! For a more graphic illustration of how much sugar you eat in a year, next time you're in a grocery store, take a stroll down to the sugar shelf. Count out twenty-seven five-pound bags of sugar. Now that's a sweet tooth!

If sugar did something good for you—other than taste good—it might not pose such a problem. But sugar contains none of the nutrients you need to grow strong and healthy—that's why it's considered "empty calories." What's worse, your liver converts sugar into fat. The *only* thing sugar does is give you a quick burst of energy. But lots of other foods provide you with longer-lasting energy—and also are healthier for you.

When you eat a piece of candy, you know you're eating sugar. But more than two-thirds of the sugar you eat comes from "hidden" sources. Guess which of the following foods contain sugar:

☆☆ **SUGAR QUIZ** ☆☆

Food	Contains sugar?	
1. Bread	Yes	No
2. Spinach	Yes	No
3. Milk	Yes	No
4. Peanut butter	Yes	No
5. Blueberry muffin	Yes	No
6. Ketchup	Yes	No
7. Orange	Yes	No
8. Mayonnaise	Yes	No
9. Hot dogs	Yes	No
10. Spaghetti sauce	Yes	No

☆☆☆

If you answered Yes to every single item, then you've certainly got sugar smarts. Each of the foods above contains *some* sugar (although a half cup of spinach only has about one gram, or one-quarter teaspoon, as does one slice of bread). Does that mean you shouldn't eat foods like oranges, milk, spinach, peanut butter and bread? Certainly not; these foods are good for you. For example, an orange may contain three and one-half teaspoons of sugar, but that's natural sugar, not refined sugar. Plus, an orange gives you lots of vitamins, especially C, as well as fiber. That's why eating fruit for your sweet tooth is so smart.

WHAT'S ALL THIS SUGAR DOING IN MY FOOD AND HOW DID IT GET THERE?

Sugar also sneaks its way into processed foods, like cereals, by using different names. If you don't know what those names are, you won't be able to recognize them on a label. *Fructose* and *glucose* are natural sugars, found in most fruits and vegetables. *Lactose* is the sugar milk contains. Refined sugar—the kind to watch out for—is often called *sucrose*. The many other faces of sugar include: maltose, malt syrup, corn syrup, corn sweetener, maple syrup, dextrose, invert sugars, molasses and honey.

Honey? But I thought honey was good for me? For a long time, the buzz about honey was that it was a healthier "sweet." It isn't. Honey may be sweeter, but, it's basically just one more form of sugar. Honey also contains more calories than sugar. Honey does have a few vitamins and minerals, unlike refined sugar, but hardly enough to do you much good. Finally, honey may be worse for your teeth since it sticks to them more easily.

ARTIFICIAL SWEETENERS: GOOD NEWS OR BAD?

In an effort to cut down on sugar, millions of Americans have switched to using artificial sweeteners, such as saccharin and aspartame, commonly called Nutra-Sweet. Artificial sweeteners *do* give you a lot of sweetness for almost *no* calories. But these are artificial chemicals we're talking about. Sugar, admittedly, brings on its own problems, like obesity and tooth decay. Artificial sweeteners don't cause either of these problems, but may trigger others. A while back, scientists found that extremely high doses of saccharin produced cancerous tumors in lab animals. This caused a "saccharin scare" for some time, but since no one proved that it does the same in people, many still use it.

Some dieticians say that one, even two artificially sweetened beverages a day probably won't do you any harm. Others disagree. But many girls and boys— many grown-ups, too—drink them in place of milk and other nutritious beverages, and that's not good. If your diet includes artificial sweeteners, try to cut back. Better yet, cut them out completely.

THE SUGAR SWING

Another side effect of refined sugar is its ability to make your energy level quickly yo-yo. Think about the last time you ate something really sugary-sweet. Soon after, you probably felt a surge of energy. But how long did that feeling last? Sugar's "quick burst" is inevitably followed by a big "boom": headaches, fatigue—even hunger. One minute you're ready to take on the school track champ! The next minute, you can barely get out of the starting blocks. Sugar is a poor choice for "fuel food"—at least if you hope to get good mileage out of your human machine.

STUCK ON SUGAR? HOW TO KICK (OR AT LEAST CONTROL) THE CRAVING.

Despite sugar's many drawbacks, many people find themselves stuck on the stuff. They're "chocoholics" and "sweetaholics." If you're hooked on sweets, know that you can always unhook yourself. Besides, who's in charge? You—or that chocolate bar?

SURVIVING SUGAR WITHDRAWAL

To break the sugar cycle, you must first eat all the good foods you should be eating. If you're full, you'll be less tempted to reach for a sweet. Save sugar for a "treat," for special events like birthdays and parties.

If your body's used to a steady sugar supply, steering clear of sweets completely is going to shake it up—at first.

You may feel tired, hungry, weak, irritable, headachy, even depressed. The first three days are the worst. After a week, the "sugar symptoms" start to abate, and should disappear completely in about three weeks.

Are cravings driving you crazy? Have some fruit with a piece of low-fat cheese instead. The carb-and-protein combination will raise your energy and sustain it.

If you do indulge, you'll be surprised to see that your sweet tooth is satisfied with less.

Curb your sweet tooth slowly—and avoid withdrawal. Just gradually reduce your sugar intake. Soon, you'll be sugar free.

HEALTHY ALTERNATIVES TO SATISFY YOUR SWEET TOOTH

Cutting back on sugar doesn't mean you have to cut back on sweetness altogether. Sweets, in moderation, can fit into your diet. The next time you're on a date, share a dessert. It's more romantic than having your own! Below are some low- and no-sugar yummies for you to make and bake yourself.

IMPORTANT SAFETY RULE:
Always get your mom's or dad's okay and, more important, their *help*, before you start cooking in the kitchen.

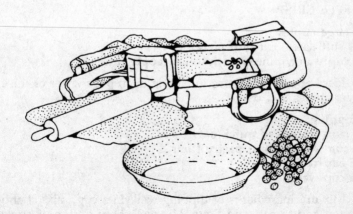

EATING PRETTY RECIPES*

CREAM PUFFS

1 cup low-fat milk
¼ lb. (1 stick) margarine, cut up
1 cup all-purpose flour
4 large eggs
1 tsp. sugar (that's it!)

Preheat oven to 400 degrees. In a saucepan over moderate heat, heat milk, margarine and sugar until mixture begins to boil and margarine is melted. Remove from heat and immediately pour in flour. Stir vigorously until dough forms a ball and leaves the side of the pan. Return to heat and stir 1 to 2 minutes to dry out dough. Remove from heat. Make a "well" in center of dough and add eggs, one at a time, beating after each addition. After the last egg, beat a minute longer, until dough is smooth and shiny. Lightly grease a baking sheet. Drop heaping tablespoons of dough onto baking sheet, making about ten 2½ inch oval mounds. Leave room between mounds for expansion. Bake 25 to 35 minutes or until golden brown. Cool in oven 1 hour with door ajar.

For a low-cal treat, fill with frozen yogurt and fresh fruit of your choice. For an extra-special treat, fill with ice cream, whipped cream, custard or pudding, and top with crushed strawberries or pineapple. *Makes 10 cream puffs.*

APPLE CRISP

6 large apples
20 soft dates, cut into pieces
1 cup water, pineapple juice, or apple juice

Place apples and dates in baking dish; pour water or juice over apples and dates.

Topping:
2 cups uncooked quick oats
1 cup whole-wheat pastry flour
½ cup vegetable oil
½ cup water

Mix dry ingredients of topping well. In a cup, mix oil and water; add to oats and flour. Mix well, pour on top of apple

110

and date mixture. Bake on bottom rack in oven at 350 degrees
for 45 minutes. If top browns too quickly, lower temperature.
Serves 6.

BANANA-OATMEAL COOKIES

3 bananas
1½ cups chopped walnuts
⅓ cup vegetable oil
1 tsp. vanilla
2 cups uncooked quick oats

In large bowl, mash bananas, then add oil, oats, walnuts
and vanilla. Drop by rounded tablespoons onto ungreased
baking sheet. Bake at 350 degrees for 20-25 minutes. Remove to
wire rack to cool. *Makes 30 cookies.*

PEANUT BUTTER BALLS

½ cup peanut butter
6 Tbsp. finely chopped dried apricots
1 Tbsp. honey (optional)
granola
¾ cup nonfat dry milk
**(You may want to substitute raisins for apricots and toasted
sesame seeds for granola.)**

Cream peanut butter and honey (if you want it) in a bowl.
Add dry milk gradually, mixing well. Stir in apricots. Shape
into 1-inch balls. Roll in granola. *Makes 24 balls.*

SUGARLESS RAISIN COOKIES

½ cup margarine
1 egg
½ to 1 cup raisins
2 tsp. vanilla
1 cup shredded, unsweetened coconut
1 cup flour
1 cup chopped walnuts
1 tsp. baking powder

Using an electric mixer, beat margarine with egg and vanilla
until smooth. In another bowl, combine flour and baking powder. Gradually add flour mixture to margarine mixture and

beat until blended. Fold in raisins, coconut and walnuts until blended. Form dough into 2 (1½ inch) rolls and wrap in wax paper or foil. Chill in freezer until firm enough to slice easily, about 2 hours. With knife, cut rolls into ¾ inch slices. Place on lightly greased baking sheet and bake at 350 degrees for 12 minutes. *Makes 2 dozen cookies.*

*All recipes courtesy of Gail Meinhold, R. D.

Health and Nutrition No-Nos

*D*rugs. Alcohol. Cigarettes. How many times have you listened patiently while someone—a parent, a friend, a teacher, a coach—says these words: "They're bad for you"? You probably hear it all the time—maybe even to the point that you're sick of it. If you're thinking to yourself, "Oh, no. Here comes another lecture," relax; that's not the goal here.

Just as you must learn to make your own choices about what foods you eat, you also have to make decisions about drugs, alcohol and cigarettes— whether they'll be a part of your life or not. No, the writer of this book does **NOT** condone the use of any of the above substances. But when you're face-to-face with such choices, **YOU** will have to be prepared to make a decision for yourself. The hope is that if you're better informed on the subject, you'll make a better, wiser (okay, we'll say it, just once), drug-free decision.

APPETITE FOR DESTRUCTION

How could anyone forget those anti-drug TV commercials such as the one that goes something like, "This is drugs. This is your brain on drugs." Screen flashes to picture of egg frying. "Any questions?"

The illustration is a vivid one, and its message is perfectly clear: Drugs, including alcohol and cigarettes, are dangerous. The truth, though, is that even in this age of the *"Just Say No"* campaign, when more and more young people are getting much needed information about substance abuse, too many pre-teens, teens and even young children are saying "yes"—and getting hooked. Obviously, some of these kids still have questions that haven't been answered. As a result, they're looking for solutions in other places—a bottle, a pill, a cigarette, you name it.

By now, most public schools, and many private ones, have made substance-abuse education a mandatory part of their curriculum. You, too, may have learned about some of the negative health effects of such habits. You're aware that all three substances—drugs, alcohol and cigarettes—not only take their toll on your physical well-being, but on your emotional well-being, too. Ultimately, these substances can **KILL** you.

114

No matter how much you already think you know about substance abuse, though, you can never know enough about what you're putting your body through when you drink, smoke or take drugs. One area most drug abuse prevention programs don't spend much time on is how these substances relate to nutrition, diet and eating habits. Let's put your knowledge to the test.

Read the statements below and decide which ones are true and which are false. Some may be a bit trickier than others, but you'll find that the answers will be thoroughly explained throughout this chapter.

☆☆ QUIZ ☆☆

Test Your Smarts About Substance Abuse

1. *Despite health warnings concerning cigarette use, more and more young people are becoming smokers.*
   True or False

2. *Cigarette smokers eat just as much as nonsmokers.*
   True or False

3. *Smoking may cause other health problems, but it does not interfere with your body getting the nutrients it needs.*
   True or False

4. *Smoking after a meal enhances the flavor of food— that's why so many people light up after a meal.*
   True or False

5. *People who abuse drugs commonly lose weight.*
   True or False

6. *Because alcohol is legal (although age restrictions for purchase/consumption exist), that must mean that it*

*does not pose that much of a threat to a person's
health.*
   True or False
7. *People who abuse drugs or alcohol generally exercise
   less.*
   True or False

Answers: 1. True 2. False 3. False 4. False 5. True
6. False 7. True

☆☆☆

   Despite the push for substance-abuse education,
more young people than ever are experimenting with
and abusing drugs, alcohol and cigarettes. With all the
serious trouble that substance abuse brings, why do
you think it's on the rise?
   The answers aren't easy. Some young people seem
to think that drugs, alcohol and cigarettes will make
their problems disappear. In fact, the opposite is true;
substance abuse eventually compounds and com-
plicates problems—and makes you feel worse, not
better.
   You're finding out that adolescence can be an awkward time. In order to feel less awkward and more
comfortable with all the changes they're going
through, some teens resort to drugs, alcohol and cigarettes as a way to be "cool." They often ignore other
activities, including school events, exercising—and
even eating—in order to spend more time using
drugs.
   Why do so many teens ignore all the warnings

about drugs, alcohol and cigarettes? It's known as the "no-way-it-can't-possibly-happen-to-me!" syndrome. You're young—and you feel like you're going to live forever. Unfortunately, drugs can not only mess up your life, they can put a quick end to it.

CIGARETTES

The warnings are printed in plain English, right on the pack where you can't miss them. So why are so many young people—even more girls than boys—lighting up? It just doesn't make sense. Smokers set themselves up for health disaster. And the younger you are when you begin smoking, the harder it usually is to quit—one more good reason not to start in the first place!

The "payoff" for puffing? A hacking cough, early facial wrinkles, dirty lungs, less resistance to illness and increased chances for both heart attacks and cancer, not to mention a shortened life span. Some payoff.

Smoking doesn't do wonders for your healthy diet, either. First, for many smokers, cigarettes may take the place of healthy, nutritious snacking. Smoking suppresses your appetite, so smokers may eat less than they should, and cut out vital nutrients in the process. Contrary to what smokers may want to believe, smoking actually desensitizes the taste buds—and does little to enhance the flavor of food. Also, smokers often have less vitamin C in their bloodstream than nonsmokers. So, there you have it. Smokers may "get the stick," but they definitely get the short end of it.

ALCOHOL

In most states, it's not even legal to drink alcohol until you're twenty-one. But because alcohol is legal in this country, many people don't think of it as a drug. Yet that's exactly what it is—a deadly drug. Alcohol kills not only those who drink it, but also the scores of innocent people drunk drivers kill on the road every year. Estimates say that at least fifty percent of all traffic accidents involve alcohol use. Despite these "sobering" statistics, alcohol is the substance more people—including young people—abuse than any other.

People can get addicted to alcohol, just like they can get addicted to other drugs. Teens and pre-teens can get hooked, too. The scariest part is that alcoholism is a serious and deadly disease, and just because you're a teen doesn't mean you can't get it. Teens and pre-teens who are problem drinkers, or who could be getting hooked on alcohol may:

- ✪ have a drink to change their mood
- ✪ drink alone, or hide their drinking from friends
- ✪ sneak a drink between classes
- ✪ feel as if they can't have "fun" without drinking

These are sure signs of alcoholism. If you or someone you know drinks like this, there's plenty of help available. Talk to your school counselor.

All the healthy food in the world won't make up for the damage you can eventually do to your system if you become an alcoholic. Alcoholics may suffer from many alcohol-related diseases such as chronic stomach problems (alcoholic gastritis, pancreatitis), liver

118

problems (cirrhosis), heart disease, nerve disease (alcoholic neuritis) and malnutrition. For your health's sake, the best thing to do is to not start drinking in the first place.

Alcohol and cigarettes may be two of the most commonly abused substances, but as you know, they aren't the only drugs out there:

MARIJUANA

Today's marijuana is a very potent drug. After smoking one marijuana joint, or cigarette, your brain activity is significantly slower. Heavy marijuana use can interfere with your menstrual cycle, and decrease sperm levels in boys. It can also weaken your body's immune system. And if you think smoking regular tobacco cigarettes is bad for your lungs, marijuana smoke is much more damaging.

COCAINE AND CRACK

These are both extremely addictive drugs. Crack is a more dangerous, less expensive kind of cocaine that is smoked. Its addictive powers are so strong that you can become addicted immediately. Even worse, crack can kill you just as quickly—the first time you use it. Regular cocaine can also prove deadly, as it has been linked both to fatal heart attacks and to seizures. Anyone who's survived cocaine addiction will tell you: It's terrible stuff. You can't say **NO** to it loudly enough.

HEROIN

Heroin has always been considered a dangerous, life-threatening drug, and now there's a new risk to using it: the fatal disease, AIDS. Heroin users inject the drug with needles, and many of them share needles, which puts them at a high risk for contracting the AIDS virus. Two death threats instead of one. Fortunately, heroin use among teens is less common than the use of other drugs.

PILLS

Certain kinds of pills, *amphetamines*, also known as "uppers," and *barbiturates*, "downers," can have a devastating effect on your body—and may even cause death. As for another group of drugs, *hallucinogens*, such as PCP and LSD, the most important thing to know about them is that they, too, can destroy your life. If there's one thing you learn from all this drug talk, it's this:

Taking drugs is one risk in life that is just not worth taking—especially since it may mean risking your life.

What about *diet pills*? Well, they're dangerous drugs, too. Some of them claim they'll help you "curb your appetite." Others promise they make you burn body fat more quickly. Some get rid of water weight—not body fat. Even if they did work, diet pills are an artificial and unsafe means of weight control. They do nothing to retrain your eating habits. Besides, if diet pills *did* work, why would so many people still be searching for the "perfect" diet? The only diet that even comes close to being perfect is a well-balanced, nutritious, healthy one.

CAFFEINE: CUTTING BACK

Every time you drink a cola or eat a piece of chocolate, you're getting more than you bargained for: It's

120

called *caffeine*. It's also found in coffee, tea and many kinds of medication. Caffeine is also a drug—a mild stimulant—something that gives you a little "lift," especially when you're tired. And while it may be tame compared to other drugs, it's still not good for you. Caffeine:

- ✪ Increases blood cholesterol levels.
- ✪ Can have a yo-yo effect on your blood sugar.
- ✪ Can irritate your stomach—it may even lead to ulcers.

Because of their size, children and young people may be more susceptible to some of caffeine's effects, especially headaches, nervousness and crankiness. If you experience any of these symptoms, it's time to call it quits with caffeine. Besides, caffeine's boost is nothing compared to the one you'll get from eating healthy.

So, avoid those nutritional no-nos, keep eating those healthy foods and you'll have a long, happy, healthy life!

SMART TALK Has It All!

Some of the best tips for fashion, fun and friendship are in the Smart Talk series. Learn how to look and feel your greatest, create your own personal style, and show the world the great new you! Smart Talk points the way:

Skin Deep
Looking Good
Eating Pretty
Feeling Fit
Finishing Touches—Manners with Style
Now You're Talking—Winning with Words
Dream Rooms—Decorating with Flair
Great Parties—How to Plan Them
How to Make (and Keep) Friends